Georg Muffat
on Performance Practice

THE TEXTS FROM

Florilegium Primum,
Florilegium Secundum,

AND

Auserlesene Instrumentalmusik

A NEW TRANSLATION WITH COMMENTARY

Edited and translated by David K. Wilson

from a collation prepared by

Ingeborg Harer, Yvonne Luisi-Weichsel, Ernest Hoetzl, and

Thomas Binkley

INDIANA UNIVERSITY PRESS

BLOOMINGTON & INDIANAPOLIS

This book is a publication of

Indiana University Press
601 North Morton Street
Bloomington, IN 47404-3797 USA

http://iupress.indiana.edu

Telephone orders 800-842-6796
Fax orders 812-855-7931
E-mail orders iuporder@indiana.edu

The paper used in this publication meets the minimum
requirements of American National Standard for Information
Sciences—Permanence of Paper for Printed Library
Materials, ANSI Z39.48-1984.

Manufactured in the United States of America

Library of Congress Cataloging-in-Publication Data

Muffat, Georg, 1653–1704.
[Essays. English. Selections]
Georg Muffat on performance practice : the texts from Florilegium primum, Florilegium
secundum, and Auserlesene Instrumentalmusik : a new translation with commentary / edited and
translated by David K. Wilson from a collation prepared by Ingeborg Harer, Yvonne Luisi-Weichsel,
Ernest Hoetzl, and Thomas Binkley.
p.   cm. — (Publications of the Early Music Institute)
Includes bibliographical references and indexes.
ISBN 0-253-21397-5 (pa : alk. paper)
1. Performance practice (Music)—Germany—17th century.   I. Wilson, David, date   II. Muffat,
Georg, 1653–1704. Suavioris harmoniae instrumentalis hyporchematicae florilegium primum.
English. Selections.   III. Muffat, Georg, 1653–1704. Florilegium, no. 2. English. Selections.   IV.
Muffat, Georg, 1653–1704. Exquisitioris harmoniae instrumentalis gravi-jucundae. English.
Selections.   V. Title.   VI. Series.

ML457 .M8313 2001
784.193—dc21

00-040998

1 2 3 4 5   06 05 04 03 02 01

To the memory of
Thomas Binkley

CONTENTS

Preface

 he project which has become this document, namely a new translation into English of the written materials published by Georg Muffat with his three volumes of instrumental ensemble music, was initiated by the late Thomas Binkley. Binkley felt that there was a need to make these materials available in English, because of their importance as a guide to performance practice; although portions of Muffat's writings have been translated and published in English, he felt that a publication which offered all the extant written material from the three publications under one cover, from a single translator, with a commentary geared toward the practical performer, would be a useful thing. In addition, the existing translations are primarily based on the French version; Binkley reasoned that since Muffat's writings were originally published in German, Italian, Latin, and French, a new translation should take into account any discrepancies which might exist between the four versions, and that the main body of the new translation might be based on the German version.

Since Binkley did not feel sufficiently well-versed in the seventeenth-century versions of these languages to make the kind of careful translation he had in mind, he arranged for a composite version in modern German, in which he was completely fluent, to be produced from which he could make a translation into English. For this work, he turned to Ingeborg Harer, Yvonne Luisi-Weichsel, and Ernest Hoetzel from the Institut für Aufführungspraxis at the Hochschule für Musik und darstellende Kunst in Graz, Austria. Harer began by rendering the original German texts (Text 1) from volumes 2, 4, and 23 of *Denkmäler der Tonkunst in Österreich* in modern German (Text 2), while seeking to preserve the original character of the text as much as possible. Next, the texts of the Italian, Latin, and French versions from DTÖ were compared with Text 2 by Harer, Luisi-Weichsel, and Hoetzel respectively, and any discrepancies in content between these versions and Text 2 were noted and translated into modern German. Finally, Harer undertook to integrate Text 2 and the translated variant readings into a single document (Text 3); she completed this work in December of 1990, and sent Text 3 to Thomas Binkley in Bloomington.

In the spring of 1994, Binkley suggested to me that I take over the task of producing an English translation based on Text 3. "It's been on my shelf for several years," he told me, "and I'm never going to do it." At that point in time, few people were aware that Binkley was dying of cancer; certainly I was not, and the significance of this remark escaped me. Binkley felt that my knowledge of modern German and my work in music of the seventeenth century made me an ideal choice to complete the project. I agreed to work on a translation and commentary, and he gave me Text 3, along with his own preliminary notes on translation.

I began translating during the summer of that year, consulting regularly with Binkley about

the character of the translation as well as the format of the final product. Binkley was interested in the creation of a translation which would be not only accurate, but readable; a dry or
pedantic translation, he argued, would be one which no one would want to read, and his goal
was to produce something which would be useful to performers. We also experimented with
various arrangements of the text on the page which would include the alternate readings from
Italian, Latin, and French without disturbing the flow of the main body of the text, finally set-
tling on a two-column approach with the alternate readings in smaller type on the right side
of the page. Binkley's reasoning on the issue of format was the same as his reasoning on the
character of the translation: if the text is too cluttered with markings or interpolations, he said,
it will be too hard to read, and no one will bother to do so. For the same reason of clarity, I
have reproduced Muffat's musical examples using music-writing software (Professional Composer 2.1), with modern signs for up- and down-bows.

My goal has been to produce a translation which is linguistically accurate, musically in-
telligible, easily readable, and still true to the tone and character of the original. In the last
month of his life, when he was already confined to bed, Binkley spoke with me on the telephone about the project and reiterated his desire that the translation be "readable," a useful,
practical document for performers. I have done my best to honor that desire while at the same
time trying to live up to the standard of scholarly excellence upon which he always insisted. I
have decided to focus my commentary on issues in Muffat's writings which pertain directly
to performance, eschewing for the moment issues which are primarily musicological in nature (issues which could be the topics of later projects).

I would like to extend a special note of thanks to Sara Colburn for her role in the comple-
tion of this project. Without her encouragement, her emotional support, and her faith in me,
to say nothing of her editorial assistance, her help in translating French terms, and her insight-
ful observations about the material, this work might never have come to print.

Thanks as well to Mary Burke for proofreading my translations of Text 3 and for her sugges-
tions, to Austin Caswell, Stanley Ritchie, Elisabeth Wright, and Wendy Gillespie for their
ongoing input and encouragement, and to Stewart Carter for making available to me a preliminary draft of his paper on Bartolomeo Bismantova's *Compendio Musicale*. My greatest
thanks and appreciation go to Thomas Binkley, to whose memory this work is dedicated.

Source Materials and Editions

1. Suavioris Harmoniæ Instrumentalis Hyporchematicæ Florilegium Primum
    (commonly called the *Florilegium Primum*)
        Published in Augsburg, 1695. Printed by Jacob Koppmayr in six part-books:[1]
- Violine
- Violetta
- Viola
- Quinta Parte
- Violone
- Basso continuo ad libitum

      Surviving complete copies:[2]
- Uppsala, University Library, Utl. instr. mus. tr. 80:1, 6 vol.
- Prague, National Museum, Music Division, II LB 35. From the library of His Highness Prince Moritz von Lobkowitz, Duke of Raudnitz an der Elbe

      Modern edition:
- Georg Muffat, *Florilegium: für Streichinstrumente, in Partitur mit unterlegtem Clavierauszug* (in two volumes), edited by Heinrich Rietsch, series: Denkmäler der Tonkunst in Österreich (Vol. 2), Vienna: Artaria, 1894–1995.

      Contents:
- Title Page
- Dedication to Johann Philipp von Lamberg
- Poem *Ad Authorem* by Michäel Alber
- Poem *An den Verfasser* by Christian Leopold Krünner
- Poem *Ad Zoilum*
- Author's Foreword to the well-meaning connoisseur
- Fifty consecutively numbered pieces, arranged into seven suites:

FASCICULUS I *EUSEBIA*

      1. Ouverture   2. Air   3. Sarabande   4. Gigue
      5. Gavotte   6. Gigue II   7. Menuett

---

[1] Inka Stampfl, *Georg Muffat Orchesterkompositionen* (Passau: Verlag Passavia, 1984), p. 32.
[2] Ibid., p. 264.

FASCICULUS II *SPERANTIS GAUDIA*

    8. Ouverture   9. Balet   10. Bourrée   11. Rondeau
    12. Gavotte   13. Menuet I   14. Menuet II

FASCICULUS III *GRATITUDO*

    15. Ouverture   16. Balet   17. Air   18. Bourrée
    19. Gigue   20. Gavotte   21. Menuet

FASCICULUS IV *IMPATIENTA*

    22. Symphonie   23. Balet   24. Canaries   25. Gigue
    26. Sarabande   27. Bourrée   28. Chaconne

FASCICULUS V *SOLLICITUDO*

    29. Ouverture   30. Allemande   31. Air   32. Gavotte
    33. Menuet I   34. Menuet II   35. Bourrée

FASCICULUS VI *BLANDITIÆ*

    36. Ouverture   37. Sarabande   38. Bourrée
    39. Chaconne   40. Gigue   41. Menuet   42. Echo

FASCICULUS VII *CONSTANTIA*

    43. Air   44. Entrée des Fraudes   45. Entrée des Insultes
    46. Gavotte   47. Bourrée   48. Menuet I   49. Menuet II
    50. Gigue

• Afterword

2. Suavioris Harmoniæ Instrumentalis Hyporchematicæ Florilegium Secundum
    (commonly called the *Florilegium Secundum*)
    Published in Passau, 1698. Printed by Georg Adam Höller in six part-books:[3]
        • Violine
        • Violetta
        • Viola
        • Quinta Parte
        • Violone
        • Basso continuo ad libitum
    Surviving complete copy:[4]
        • Prague, National Museum, Music Division, II LB 35. From the library of

---

[3] Ibid., p. 32.
[4] Ibid., p. 265.

His Highness Prince Moritz von Lobkowitz, Duke of Raudnitz an der Elbe

Modern edition:

- Georg Muffat, *Florilegium: für Streichinstrumente, in Partitur mit unterlegtem Clavierauszug* (in two volumes), edited by Heinrich Rietsch, series: Denkmäler der Tonkunst in Österreich (Vol. 4), Vienna: Artaria, 1894–1995.

Contents:

- Title page
- Note concerning the four-language introductory materials (Viola, Quinte parte, and Basso continuo only)
- Errata
- Instructions to the bookbinder
- Dedication to Johann Traugott von Kufstein and Liebgott von Kufstein
- Poem, *Ad Authorem*, by Christian Leopold Krünner
- Poem, *Ad Zoilum*
- Foreword
- First Remarks. The performance of the ballets in the Lullian-French manner.
- Sixty-two consecutively numbered pieces, arranged in eight suites:

FASCICULUS I *NOBILIS JUVENTUS*[5] (D MINOR)

1. Ouverture   2. Entrée d'Espagnols   3. Air pour des Hollandois   4. Gigue pour des Anglois   5. Gavotte pour des Italiens   6. I. Menuet pour des François   7. II. Menuet

FASCICULUS II *LAETA POËSIS* (G MAJOR)

8. Ouverture   9. Les Poëtes   10. Jeunes Espagnoles   11. Autre pour les mêmes   12. Les Cuisiniers   13. Le Hachis   14. Les Marmitons

FASCICULUS III *ILLUSTRES PRIMITIÆ* (A MINOR)

15. Ouverture   16. Galliarde   17. Courante 18. Sarabande   19. Gavotte   20. Passacaille   21. Bourée 22. Menuet   23. Gigue

FASCICULUS IV *SPLENDIDÆ NUPTIÆ* (D MAJOR)

24. Ouverture   25. Les Païsans   26. Canaries   27. Les

---

[5] In the "Index of the Partitas in this work," Muffat translated these Latin titles into German; I have provided English translations for each (see p. 62).

Cavalliers   28. I. Menuet   29. Rigodon pour des Jeunes Païsannes
Poitevines   30. II. Menuet

FASCICULUS V COLLIGATI MONTES (G MINOR)

31. Ouverture   32. Entrée des Maîtres d'armes   33. Autre Air pour
les mêmes   34. Un Fantôme   35. Les Ramonneurs   36. Gavotte
pour les Amours   37. I. Menuet, pour l'Hymen   38. II. Menuet

FASCICULUS VI GRATI HOSPITES (A MAJOR)

39. Caprice   40. Gigue   41. Gavotte   42. Rigodon dit le
solitaire   43. Contredanse   44. Bourée de Marly imitée
45. Petite Gigue

FASCICULUS VII NUMÆ ANCILE (E MINOR)

46. Ouverture   47. Entrée de Numa   48. Autre air pour le
même   49. Traquenard pour de Jeunes Romains   50. II. Air pour
les mêmes   51. Balet pour les Amazones   52. I. Menuet pour les
susdittes   53. II. Menuet

FASCICULUS VIII INDISSOLUBILIS AMICITIA (E MAJOR OR E-FLAT MAJOR)

54. Ouverture   55. Les Courtisans   56. Rondeau   57. Les
Gendarmes   58. Les Bossus   59. Gavotte   60. Sarabande pour
le Genie de l'Amitié   61. Gigue   62. Menuet

- Index of the Partitas in This Work
- Index of the Author's Works in Print

**3. Exquisitioris Harmoniæ Instrumentalis Gravi-Jucundæ Selectus Primus . . .
Auserlesene mit ernst und lust gemengte Instrumentalmusik**
(commonly called the *Auserlesene Instrumentalmusik*)
Published in Passau, 1701. Printed by Maria Margaretha Höllerin in eight part-
books:[6]
- Violino I Concertino
- Violino II Concertino
- Basso Continuo e Violoncino Concertino
- Violino I Concerto Grosso
- Violino II Concerto Grosso
- Viola I Concerto Grosso

---

[6] Stampfl, p. 32.

- Viola II Concerto Grosso
- Violone e Cembalo Concerto Grosso

Surviving complete copy:[7]

- Prague, National Museum, Music Division, II LB 34. From the library of His Highness Prince Ferdinand Zdenko von Lobkowitz of Raudnitz an der Elbe

Modern edition:

- Georg Muffat, *Sechs Concerti grossi I, nebst einem Anhange: Auswahl aus Armonico Tributo (1682): Auserlesene mit ernst und lust gemengte Instrumentalmusik (1701)*, edited by Erwin Luntz, series: Denkmäler der Tonkunst in Österreich (Vol. 23), Graz: Akademische Druck- und Verlagsanstalt, 1959 (reprint; originally published Vienna, 1904). Includes concerti II, IV, V, X–XII.

Georg Muffat, *Armonico tributo (1682)*; *Exquisitioris harmoniae instrumentalis gravi, jucundae selectus primus (1701): concerti grossi, zweiter teil*, edited by Erich Schenk, series: Denkmäler der Tonkunst in Österreich (Vol. 89), Vienna: Österreichischer Bundesverlag, 1953. Includes concerti I, III, VI–IX.

Contents:

- Title Page in Latin
- Title Page in Vernacular (Violino I Concertino=German, Violino II Concertino=Italian, Violone, e Cembalo Concerto Grosso=French)
- Portrait of Dedicatee Maximilian Ernst
- Dedication to Maximilian Ernst
- Foreword
- Twelve Concertos:

   Concerto I *Bona Nova*[8] (D minor)
      Sonata, Ballo, Grave, Aria, Giga
   Concerto II *Cor Vigilans* (A major)
      Sonata, Corrente, Grave, Gavotta, Rondeau
   Concerto III *Convalescentià* (B minor)
      Sonata, Aria, Grave, Giga I, Giga II
   Concerto IV *Dulce somnium* (G minor)
      Sonata, Sarabanda, Grave-Adagio, Aria, Borea
   Concerto V *Sæculum* (D major)
      Sonata, Allemanda, Grave, Gavotta, Menuet

---

[7] Ibid., p. 266

[8] In the "Index of the Concertos Contained in This Work," Muffat translated these Latin titles into German; I have provided English translations for each (see p. 79).

Part One

Introduction

Chapter 1

Biographical Sketch of Georg Muffat

Early Years

𝒪n the early seventeenth century, Georg Muffat's paternal ancestors left Scotland to escape religious persecution. (Indeed, the name Moffat is a common one in Scotland.) Life for Scottish Catholics had become increasingly difficult since Catholicism was officially outlawed by the Scottish Parliament in 1560, following the collapse of an alliance between Scotland and Catholic France. During the course of the next half century, Catholic clergy were imprisoned or banished, and Catholic laity were fined for failing to attend Protestant worship. King James VI (who also ruled England as James I) renewed and strengthened the anti-Catholic legislation enacted by Elizabeth I, and in 1604, following an unsuccessful attempt by militant Catholics to blow up Parliament and the royal family (the "Gunpowder Plot"), Parliament passed laws forbidding Catholics from practicing medicine or law, prohibiting them from traveling more than five miles from their homes, and imposing similar restrictions. It is not surprising that many Scottish Catholics chose to emigrate to escape this situation.

Georg Muffat was baptized on June 1, 1653, in the town of Megève in Savoy. (His mother's family was French.) When Muffat was a boy, his family moved from Savoy to the Alsatian town of Schlettstadt.

At the age of ten, he was sent to Paris to study music. The identity of his teachers in Paris is unclear; Muffat is assumed to have studied with Jean-Baptiste Lully, which is perhaps a reasonable assumption considering Lully's preeminence in the musical life of France at that time. However, Muffat wrote:

> For six years, along with other music studies, I avidly pursued this manner which was flowering in Paris at that time under the most famous Jean-Baptiste Lully. (F1, Foreword)

The sense of this passage is that the manner of playing Muffat described (which he avidly pursued) was flowering under Lully, not that he was pursing this manner (which was flowering in Paris) under Lully. He later wrote,

> I had my start in France with the most experienced masters of this art of music. (F1, Dedication)

If Muffat did indeed study with Lully, it seems surprising that he would not say so unequivo-cally. In any case, Muffat lived in Paris between 1663 and 1669, during the period of Lully's influence, and no doubt studied music with teachers who were involved in the Lullian style, if not with Lully himself.

At the age of 16, Muffat left Paris and returned to Alsace. He enrolled at a Jesuit college in the town of Séléstat (a center of humanist erudition) in 1669, and in 1671 he was a "Rheto-ricus" at the Jesuit Gymnasium in the nearby town of Molsheim, where he also obtained a position as organist to the chapter-in-exile of the Strasbourg Cathedral (the cathedral being Protestant at the time).

Years of Travel

In the 1660s and 1670s, after France's victory in the Thirty Years' War, Louis XIV sought to capitalize on France's prosperity to expand his Empire. He began by invading the Spanish Netherlands (now Belgium), a move which caused England and Sweden to unite with Hol-land against him in the so-called "Triple Alliance." The war officially ended a year later with the Treaty of Aix-la-Chapelle. Within a few years, however, Charles II of England agreed in the secret Treaty of Dover to join with France against Holland, and Sweden also withdrew from the Triple Alliance, since it required France's help in its struggle with Germany and Denmark. Louis then invaded Holland, joined by armies from England. But by 1674, the English Par-liament had forced Charles II to make peace with Holland, and both Austria and Brandenburg sent armies to oppose France. That year, in an attempt to starve Holland into submission, Louis' armies devastated the provinces of the Palatinate and Lorraine, and portions of Alsace.

By this time, Muffat had seen that war was on the way. In 1674, barely ahead of the devas-tation wrought by Louis' armies, he entered law school at the University of Ingolstadt in Ba-varia. The study of law must not have appealed to him, for he soon moved to Vienna to look for work as a musician. Muffat might very well have known three famous Johanns (Pachelbel, Schmelzer, and Kerll) during the few years he was in Vienna. Emperor Leopold I reportedly appreciated his talents, but did not offer him a position; so he moved again, this time to Prague. It was in Prague that Muffat wrote his violin sonata, which is his earliest surviving work and is dated July 2, 1677. Despite Muffat's years of study in France, the sonata owes more to the German style represented by Schmelzer and Kerll than it does to the French dance style. Like German and Italian instrumental sonatas of the seventeenth century, the piece consists of a single movement with contrasting internal sections, and the contrapuntal writing is certainly more characteristic of the German style than of the French.

Salzburg and Rome

In 1678, Muffat left Prague (a scant three years before plague killed around 83,000 in that city) and became employed as cathedral organist and chamber musician (*Domorganist* and *Kammerdiener*) at the court of Maximilian Gandolf von Küenberg, Archbishop of Salzburg. Max Gandolf was a patron of music; Heinrich Biber and Andreas Hofer, both respected mu-sicians, were employed by him as well. Muffat's conditions of employment must have been quite liberal, for within a few years he was granted a sabbatical leave to journey to Rome and learn the Italian musical style. In the Foreword to his *Auserlesene Instrumentalmusik*, Muffat wrote this of his Roman sojourn:

> The first thoughts of this ingenious mixture came to me some time ago in Rome, where I was learning the Italian style on the keyboard under the world-famous Bernardo Pasquini, when I heard with great excitement and amazement some concertos of the talented Arcangelo Corelli performed most beautifully and with great precision by a large number of instrumentalists. As I noticed the many contrasts in those pieces, I composed some of these present concertos, and I tried them out in the home of the above-mentioned Arcangelo Corelli (to whom I feel greatly obliged for generously conveying to me many useful observations concerning this style); and with his approval, I was the first to bring some samples of this hitherto unknown harmony to Germany.

When he returned to Salzburg from Rome in 1682, Muffat published a collection of five chamber sonatas in the Italian style; the work was titled *Armonico Tributo*. These sonatas were a fusion of the Corellian style he had learned in Rome and the Lullian style he had learned in Paris. He wrote,

> I strove to moderate the melancholy Italian affects with the French festivity and beauty in such a way that the one might not be too dark and pompous, nor the other too free and boisterous. (*Auserlesene Instrumentalmusik*, Dedication)

These works contain some very Corelli-like moments which feature rich harmonies and somber emotional characters or "affects," but also contain some light and energetic French-sounding dances.

Until 1690, Muffat and his wife, Anna Elisabeth, remained at the Salzburg court, where six of their eight children were born. When Max Gandolf died in 1687, Johann Ernst von Thun was appointed Archbishop in his place. Johann Ernst did not have the same regard for music as his predecessor, and in fact hated all things French. Muffat may have already been planning a collection of instrumental works in the French ballet style (what would become his *florilegia*); if so, he would have found the court of Johann Ernst to be an unfavorable climate for such works. Muffat may have intended a reference to this animosity toward the French style in the dedication to Johann Philipp von Lamberg, Prince-Bishop of Passau, of the *Florilegium Primum*:

> Had these flowers been set out and planted in some other place, they could never have prospered; the roots would have been all but smothered, either because of harmful shade from envious branches, or through the spite of awful storms, had not Your Esteemed Grace shown them favor and freed them from the sand and the unfruitful clods, and set them out in his Passau garden bed.

Several years earlier, in 1684, Muffat's Salzburg colleague Heinrich Ignaz Franz von Biber had been promoted to the position of *Hofkapellmeister*; even though Muffat retained his church position, no Salzburg church compositions of his are known, and his name does not appear in the protocol books of the cathedral. Frustrated by his dim prospects in Salzburg for advancement and for support of the musical projects he wished to undertake, Muffat began to look for other employment. In January of 1690, at the age of 36, Muffat traveled to Augsburg to attend the coronation of Archduke Joseph, eldest son of the Holy Roman Emperor, Leopold I. While he was there, he personally presented to Leopold the book of organ toccatas, *Apparatus Musico-Organisticus*, which Muffat had dedicated to him. It is likely that during the festivities he arranged to enter the service of Prince-Bishop Johann Philipp von Lamberg in the city of Passau, because early that year he became *Hofkapellmeister* (director of music at the court) in Passau.

Passau

As *Hofkapellmeister*, Muffat had a variety of musical duties. On church holidays and political birthdays, he was responsible for providing an afternoon *Galatafel* (festive table music) with a large ensemble, and on Sundays, as well as two or three times during the week, he was to provide table music with a small ensemble. Chamber music was performed after the evening meal, and occasionally the Prince-Bishop would be entertained by his musicians aboard his barge. Several times a year, the Prince-Bishop would hold a ball for the nobles of Passau, and Muffat provided music for dancing and entertainment. Various theatrical productions were presented each year which required music. And, when the Prince-Bishop traveled to Regensburg to attend the Reichstag, a sojourn of several months, he would invariably travel with his *Hofmusik*, for his own entertainment and for the prestige of being accompanied by an entourage.

Despite what must have been a busy schedule as *Hofkapellmeister*, Muffat began soon after his arrival to undermine Passau's *Domkapellmeister* (director of church music), Johann Georg Straßer, eventually supplanting Straßer in 1692 and becoming music director at both the court and the chapel, effectively consolidating his musical authority in Passau. Two more children were born to Muffat and his wife in Passau, the first on April 25, 1690, soon after Muffat's arrival.

It was during his years in Passau that Muffat published three large collections of ensemble music. *Florilegium Primum* and *Florilegium Secundum*, or "First and Second Bouquets," were published in 1695 and 1698 respectively, and consisted of dance suites in the French or "Lullian" style which he had learned as a child in Paris. *Auserlesene Instrumentalmusik*, or "Select Instrumental Music, both serious and light-hearted," published in 1701, was a collection of Italian-style *concerti grossi*, several of which were re-workings of the *Armonico Tributo* sonatas.

In the early years of the eighteenth century, western Europe was embroiled in the War of Spanish Succession. When Charles II of Spain (a Hapsburg, like Leopold I) died in November of 1700, he had designated Philip, Duke of Anjou (a Bourbon, like Louis XIV) as his heir. Louis announced his support of Philip V, and most of the other western European powers at first assented. Leopold, however, opposed the succession, believing that he, a Hapsburg, should rightfully inherit the Spanish crown. The other European nations began to fear the power of a hypothetical union of France and Spain after Louis decided to include Philip V in the line of succession for the crown of France. The war which ensued pitted France, Spain, Cologne, and Bavaria against the Holy Roman Empire and most of the rest of Europe.

In 1703, Passau was besieged by the army of Maximilian Emmanuel, Elector of Bavaria, as part of a push by Bavarian and French troops to subdue Vienna, the Imperial capital. On January 11, 1704, after a day-long bombardment, the city fell, and was occupied by Bavarian soldiers. Muffat died on February 23 of that year; it is unclear whether his death so soon after the occupation of Passau was a direct result of that occupation. However, it is clear from Muffat's writings that two years earlier, when the *Auserlesene Instrumentalmusik* was published, he fully expected to continue composing and publishing music:

> If this work is benevolently accepted, the third Bouquet, which indulges in many other works still more unusual, and is arranged as much for the enjoyment of the ear as for theoretical usefulness, should soon follow, if Almighty God graciously lends me life and strength. (*Auserlesene Instrumentalmusik*, Index)

We might therefore conclude that if war had not finally caught up with him, he might have left us additional musical and theoretical works.

Part Two

Translations

Chapter 2

Texts from
Florilegium Primum,
1695

[TITLE PAGE]

SUAVIORIS HARMONIÆ
INSTRUMENTALIS HYPORCHEMATICÆ
FLORILEGIUM PRIMUM

First Bouquet of
instrumental dance
pieces in lovely harmony

Bouquet of lovely ballet pieces,

F=I=L: + First
F=I: +in the sweetest of
instrumental harmony.

consisting of fifty selected pieces, specifically modeled on
the current Ballet style and divided into seven different keys,
gathered together and diligently arranged for four or five
strings, together with the *Basso continuo* (if you wish).

F: Containing 50 pieces
selected for the violins and
composed according to the
newest method that is
beginning to blossom. They
can be played with four or
five parts, with *Basso
continuo* if one will. They
are divided into seven suites
or "bouquets" in various
keys. I: 50 *modulationi* of
collected melodies L:
arranged like flowers
according to their keys, with
well-fitting passages for four
or five strings, together with
Basso Continuo, if desired
for excitement

Humbly dedicated to the most venerable and illustrious
Count and Lord, Johann Philipp, Bishop, Prince of the
Holy Roman Empire for Passau, and Count of Lamberg,
with the sincerest desire for the continued success of his
ever-blooming and glorious government, by Georgio
Muffat, the highest of his Esteemed Grace's tutors of
choirboys and pages.

Printed by Jacob Koppmayr, 1695. Available for sale from
Wilhelm Pannecker, Bookseller.

The title, dedication, and Foreword of this work can be
found in German in the violin part, in Italian in the alto
and tenor viola parts, and in French in the *violetta* and
violone parts.

G: + (*Viola* and *Quinta
Parte*)

[Dedication to Johann Philipp von Lamberg]

Most Venerable, Most Illustrious
Imperial Prince, Most Gracious Lord:

F: My Lord.
I: Most Venerable Lord.
L: Most Venerable, Most
Illustrious and Charitable
Lord.

   In truth, I owe this my bouquet to none other than Your
Esteemed Grace, through whose benevolent influence these
flowers began not only to flourish,

F: this first bouquet of my
airs
I: this first selection of my
Arias and Balletts
L: this bouquet of my
modulationum

but also to bloom and to gently grow. Music and flowers
have this in common, that they fear shadows and cold,

F=L: not only to blossom,
but also to grow and become
strong
L: are favored and grow

but with the benefit of light and warmth they grow and are
sustained. Had these flowers been set out and planted in
some other place, they could never have prospered; the
roots would have been all but smothered, either because of
harmful shade from envious branches, or through the spite
of awful storms, had not Your Esteemed Grace shown them
favor and freed them from the sand and the unfruitful clods,
and set them out in his Passau garden bed.
Upon this happy planting,
I soon found myself quite covered with goodness,

F: omit "from . . . branches"

I: gardens

F: + , my Lord
I: immediately
L: pampers

just as the goodness of the air and the earth
yields itself up to the flowers.

F: covered with all those
things that the sweetness of
the air and fertility of the
earth contribute to the good
of the flowers
L: + freely
L: you

The light I received from
Your Esteemed Grace,
in that you have
deigned to grace me with the office of
Kapellmeister;
and because you believed I could accomplish something in
addition to music, you gave me the prospect of
having your pages graciously entrusted
to me.

I: + , Most Gracious Prince,
L: decorate

F: + perhaps
L: + the Prefecture of
L: omit "graciously"

This same graciousness has provided the new, cool, most necessary juice of life, in that it has provided my art with essential assistance and my work with rich support and comfort, through the magnanimous influences of your generosity. Your Esteemed Grace has with one word given these flowers such burgeoning strength, by mercifully warming and watering them, that they will abundantly multiply and grow into a bush, and become a bouquet.

However, just as the first enticement of the gardens is the diversity of the plants and flowers, and as the excellence and general felicity of great heroes, to be sure, seems to result from many intertwined virtues, I have taken the view that in the obedient service which Your Esteemed Grace, as a prince of wisdom and virtue, deserves, I dare not employ only a single style or method, but rather the most skillful mixture of styles I can manage through my experience in various countries.

Not only one style, but a collection of the best styles of various nations would be appropriate in order to amuse you with different forms of music and manners of playing. From Your Esteemed Grace, whose consummate understanding is achieved through long experience with the court and business, I have no fear of the measured attacks of those evil or weak souls who condemn me. Since I had my start in France with the most experienced masters of this art of music, I realize that I could be accused of favoring that nation more than is appropriate,

and in this time of war with France I could be considered unworthy of the kindly disposed ear of the Germans. Truly I have other thoughts than: *Ære ciere viros, Martemque accendere cantu.*[1] The weapons of war and the reasons for them are far from me;

F:+ the light, F=I=L: + essential to the young plants

I: omit "with one word"
L: power to grow

F: + , fame,

F: in order to have the honor of Your Esteemed Grace's favor
I: since you are a prince of diverse wisdom
L: For you, a prince of many-formed wisdom and virtue,

L: not only one method, but the teachings of the greatest variety of civilized cultures would be appropriate

I: censure
F: learned the basics of music
F: too strong an inclination towards that nation could be falsely construed of me
I: omit "and in . . . France"
F: the kind disposition

L: the reason for weapons
F: My profession is a great distance from the noise of weapons, and the affairs of state which they must take up

[1] To spur on the sound of arms, or to encourage the god Mars to join battle.

notes, strings, and lovely musical tones dictate my course,
and as I mix the French manner
with the German and Italian,
I do not begin

F: omit "lovely"; + I practice
sweet harmony
I: I busy myself with the
study of a lovely symphony
L: the sweet work of the
symphony occupies me
L: French modulations

a war, but perhaps rather
a prelude to the unity,
the dear peace, desired by all the peoples.
If Your Esteemed Grace loves peace, Your Esteemed Grace,
as a son of peace, will scorn music neither as a herald nor as
an escort, since peace first saw the light of day in the general
joy of the Peace of Münster, through the efforts of the
ambassadors as well as the faithful accomplishments of His
Excellency, late father of Your Esteemed Grace, under the
unanimous aspects of so many great constellations. If the
stars follow their orbits through an accord (*concentum enim
coeli dormire quie faciet?*[2]), so these concordant
constellations can only have communicated pure
peace and accord.

L: omit "a prelude to"
L: harmony

F: in the manner of a
harmonic concert
I: harmony
L: through certain
modulations

Your Esteemed Grace is therefore nourished and inspired,
and in himself combines things which are often opposite
and rarely found together: things such as the ornament of
the church and the brilliance of the court, generosity and
frugality, work and pleasure, the love and the fear of your
subjects,

F: Your Esteemed Grace
therefore can receive
through such a favorable
constellation only the spirit
of peace and accord, with
the spirit of life.
L: . . . can bring out no other
spirit than that of peace and
accord
L: those who belong to you
L: wisdom

reason in counsel,
agility in action, the reverence of
a superior, and the magnificence of a lord
with wonderful skill; because of this abundance of virtues,
we can hope that heaven will not swerve from the wishes of
Your Esteemed Grace's church and bishopric. May heaven
bestow on you not only the pleasant tones of my music, but
also a lively accord of body and soul, a glorious government
in whose repute you may rejoice, and the praises of history,
perpetually maintained for countless years to come.
Thus subjects himself to Your Esteemed Grace, your most
humble and obedient servant,
Georg Muffat.

I: Prelate
L: integrity
L: Upperworld

F: my Muse
L: harmony
L: of the spirit for numerous
years
F: These are the burning
wishes, with great respect, of
L: Thus praises . . .

[2] who might still the heavenly song?

The Author's Foreword
to the Well-Meaning
Connoisseur

Here you have the pieces I composed in Salzburg
before I came to Passau, organized mostly
in the French Ballet style,

now presented for your pleasure
and your judgement,
O well-meaning connoisseur.
I have been induced, through the frequent entreaty of good
friends and the approval of the most important musicians,
both Italian and German, to publish these pieces that have
been enjoyed by princes and commended by nobles. I have
acceded to their petition all the more happily because I

sensed that this manner of playing is gradually becoming
fashionable in Germany.
For six years, along with other music studies, I avidly
pursued this style which was flowering in Paris at that time
under the most famous Jean-Baptiste Lully. I was perhaps
the first to introduce this style, not unpleasantly, to
many celebrated musicians when I returned from France to
Alsace; from there I was driven out by the last war to Austria
and Bohemia, and afterwards to Salzburg and Passau.
However, since the ballet compositions of the above-
mentioned Lully, or other such composers, because of their
flowing and natural motion, completely avoid irregular runs,
frequent and ill-sounding leaps,

and all other artifice, they had the misfortune to be
at first poorly received in these countries by many
of our violinists, who at that time were more interested in
the number of unusual devices and artifices
in the music than in grace.
Therefore these pieces, when performed from time to time

F: Foreword to the Reader or
connoisseur of music.
I: To the well-meaning
Reader, connoisseur of
music.
L: + of the Muses.
F: +, my dear reader,
I: *modulationi*
I: arranged in the style of
Ballets.
L: arranged in the style of
dances in the French
manner
F: omit "O . . . connoisseur".

L: + of the muses

L: I wanted after all to
accede, indeed, all the more
happily
F=I=L: style
L: among the Germans
L: musical arts

F: + of good taste
F: Vienna in Austria
F: Prague
I: On my return from France
I gave a few samples of this
in Alsace. Driven out by the
last war, I was perhaps the
first who brought such ideas
to Vienna, then to Prague
and finally to Salzburg and
Passau, where the musicians
of perfected taste found these
ideas not unpleasant.
L: other artifices
L: and later

I: + and harmony

by musicians unfamiliar with the French manner or envious
of foreign art, were robbed of their correct
tempi and graces. However, these pieces were later
performed with a more splendid perfection,

first in Austria
by some foreign violinists, and soon thereafter by the
excellent musicians of the Serene Electors of Bavaria, and
thus they were considered more sophisticated. Many then
began to seek out this music, in order to become familiar
with the music so appreciated by the Lords and Princes,
in order to form better opinions
and to become accustomed to its manner
and grace. And without any doubt they
found it true, what a particularly clever Lord once said to
me with regard to this style, namely that what they learned
intellectually was more difficult
than that which they might have learned
for the pleasure of the ear.

Thus, because the thoughtless condemnation
of the aforementioned ballet style has gradually abated,
so I thought with all the more confidence to come forward
with my pieces, simple as they are, since
they need the art and favor of the
violinists all the more because of their simplicity,

so that they they may safely emerge.
It seems unnecessary to give the reason for the name of each
partita, for the names differ from one another only in the
circumstances surrounding their origin; in the end they are
indeed named according to a state of mind.
    It remains still for me to remind the musician
inexperienced in this style that
when the notes are marked in the following way,
play the first time up to the repetition sign,
but the second time completely leave out those notes
and instead begin at the repetition sign.

The sign ⅜, which may be found near the beginning or after
the repetition sign, identifies the note with which to begin,
leaving out all previous notes. This must also be observed

L: + it occured that
I: or people who disdain the
style for other reasons
L: or those who hate the
foreign manner

F=I: Vienna
F: musicians

I: omit "considered more
sophisticated"
L: + a great
I: began to form a better
opinion of this music

L: wise
L: most cleverly
L: + of music
F: + previously
F=I: more artful and more
difficult.
L: of greater and more
difficult art
F: and refusal
F: method

L: of this style

F: musicians
I: players
L: dancers
F: + In the end

F: and from the other pieces

F: my
F: certain conventions of
repetitions that are common
in this style.
L: in certain practices of this
style
F: according to the usual
practice

even if the sign is found nearly in the middle of the second
part, or somewhat further from the end. However, I found
the practice of some to be not unpleasant, which is to repeat
still a third time, beginning from the aforementioned sign
after the second part has been played completely.
The musicians should decide this before the performance.
The beat or measure indicated by the sign 2¢ must,
because it is divided into two, be once again as fast as a
measure under the sign **C**, which one divides in four.
Further, the tempo of those pieces named Ouverture,
Prelude and Symphonie,

F=I=L: not too far from the
end I: + of an Aria

L: Besides, the measure,
F=I: half again as fast
L: + usually
I: Sonate
L: in the Preludes,
Symphonies and those
melodies called Overtures
I: + grave
F: + in my view, almost

if they are marked 2, should be rather slow;
the Ballet, however, should be more lively,
although still slower than it would be if marked ¢. Under the
last sign ¢, one must not hurry in the Gavotte as one does in
the Bourée. Further, when the measure is marked 2 and is
taken very slowly in two, the value of the notes is nearly the
same as it would be with the Italians under the sign **C**, where
the measure is marked Presto and divided in four. The only
difference between these is that in the latter case a series of
eighth notes, ♪♪♪♪ etc. are not played dotted, as they would
be in the former case because of the better manner, ♪.♪♪.♪
but in equal time.

L: speed up
F: = (as I said)

F: elegance of the
performance
L: rigidly

The *Symphonie* of the fourth
Partita offers an example of this.
As for the other markings, in $\frac{3}{2}$ the measure is
quite held back, while in $\frac{3}{4}$ it is more lively,
except that in Sarabands and Airs it is a bit slower.
In the Rondeau the measure is lively; in the Minuets,
Courantes and many others, and none the less in the
Fugues attached to the Overtures, it is very fresh.
The other pieces, called Gigues and Canaries,
must be played the fastest of all,
no matter how they are marked.

F: strictly one like the other
F=I: + called *Impatientia*
L: Under the other signs,
$\frac{3}{2}$ is very slow
F: grave
F: + but finally

F: the most fresh without
being too fast.
L: brisk, without rushing
L: dances
F: + finally

If you, dear connoisseur,

I: + After this Foreword
L: + After you have learned
all of this, dear reader and
connoisseur of music
L: well-meaning reader

wish to take up this my *Florilegium primum*,
and to shelter it from the jealous and envious,
then forgive my mistakes and those that have crept in at the
printing. Expect that which is promised at the end of this
work. Farewell, and wish him well who has attempted to
deserve your favor.

I: this first selection of such
compositions
F: omit "and to . . . envious"

F: + and happily

To the Author[3]

Whence is it granted to you to present the
    bees with such a honey-rich flower in
    which to delight (themselves)?
How is it that you so skillfully govern the
    dancers?
And brings their measured steps into good
    order?
What has brought you so long in your
    Prince's favor?
You are silent; and so I say, it is your
    great art.
Apollo crowns you, and shows you his favor,
For you open the pathway for the very Muses
    themselves.
His efforts are well repaid, whoever learns to
    fiddle in this way,
For he can lead everyone who hears it to the
    dance;
Even I am one of those who must attest that
    your measure and your beat have taught
    my foot
To glide up and down and turn in
    pirouettes
Now the cadence, quite finished, like the
    fate of Life, to stand still.
What otherwise must be brought so
    laboriously from Paris your art has long
    since replaced, here and in Vienna.
Thanks be to you, Georg, go forth with gifts
    of flowers,
When friend and foe scent them, they will be
    able to refresh themselves,
Take up these seven nosegays, whoever
    would be a virtuoso,
The usefulness of it is certain, I pledge.
Thus sings and leaps Christian Leopold
    Krünner, Chamberservant and Dance
    Master to His Esteemed Grace of Passau.

An den Verfasser

Woher wird dir vergönnt, den Immen
    aufzusetzen So honigreiche Blum, darinn
    sich zuergetzen?
Was macht, daß du so kühn die Tantzer
    gleichsam zwingst?
Und ihre Regl Schritt in gute Ordnung
    bringst?
Was hat dich längst gesetzt in deines Fürsten
    Gunst?
Du schweigst, und ich thu sagen, das sei dein
    große Kunst.
Apollo kränzt dich, und ist dir zugethan,
Weil seinen Musen selbst eröffnen thust die
    Bahn.
Die Müh ist wohl verkaufft, wer so lernt
    Geigen rühren,
Kan jeden, der es hört, behend zum Tantze
    führen,
Selbst ich von denen bin, der es bezeugen
    muß, Daß dein *Mesur* und *Takt*, mir
    glehrnet hab mein
Fuß Zu schleiffen ab und auf die *Piroueten*
    drehen
Jetzt die *Cadenze* ganz aus gleich Lebens loß
    zu stehen.
Was aus Pariß sonst her man holen mußt mit
Müh Schon längst ersetzet hat dein Kunst zu
    Wienn und hie.
Georg dir sei gedankt, fahr fort mit Blumen-
    Gaben,
Wann Freund und Feind sie rücht, wird
    können sich dran laben, Nemt sieben
    Büschlein an, wer *Virtuos* will sein,
Der Nutz daraus ist gewiß, ich stell zum
    Bürg mich ein.
Also singt und springt Christian Leopold
    Krünner, Hochfürstl. Passauischer
    Cammer-Diener und Tantzmeister

---

[3] The translation of poetry is a very different undertaking than the translation of prose. For that
reason, and because these poems are given only German, I have chosen to show the original
German text in the right-hand column, for comparison with my translation in the left-hand column.

Ad Zoilum[4]

Your barbs, sarcastic people, I ignore, with
    reason alone do I seek to prove my case,
For as is your mouth and your taste, so is also
    your feedbag.
If I offer an ass even the prettiest
    of flowers,
He will disdain them, because to him the
    thistle tastes better.

Ad Zoilum

Dein Stachel, Spöttler, acht ich schlecht,
    Nur bey Verstand such ich mein Recht,
Dann wie dein Maul und der Geschmack,
    Also ist auch dein Futter-Sack.
Ob schon ich halt dem Esel-Thier Die aller-
    schönste Blumen für,
Acht er derselben sich nicht sehr, Weil ihm
    die Distel schmecket mehr.

---

[4] "To Zoilus"—In Classical literature, Zoilus was a critic and detractor. Hence, "To the Critic."

Afterword

Friendly connoisseur,
I intended to append
to these ballets
some remarks which might not displease you concerning
their performance, to encourage the higher advancement of
the art of music in our Germany, its improved progress and
its further brilliance; I promised in my *Apparatus Musico-
Organistico*, which five years ago I placed in the most serene
hands of our unconquerable Emperor Leopold at the time
of the royal coronation,

to include something noteworthy and useful
in all of my works.

However, because of the short time in which
I was forced to complete this work,
the above-mentioned remarks
could not be appropriately prepared,
so I have postponed them to be appended
to the *Florilegio Secundo*,
in the same manner as this work,
which should follow soon
if the current one finds
favor.

F: My dear reader
I: Friendly reader
I: partitas of ballets
L: certain

I: my work containing
toccatas with the title.
I: our Holy Imperial Majesty
I: coronation of the Roman
King
I: theoretical
L: each

F: I always shall include a
small theoretical treatise with
each work that I publish.
F: I intended to append to
these pieces a few remarks of
mine that perhaps will not be
offensive to you, concerning
the perfection of music, and
the most delicate way to play
it well and with greater
agility, all to the fame of our
Germany. I promised this in
my book of organ pieces
called *Apparatus Musico-
Organistico*, which I had the
honor to dedicate to, and
place in the most serene
hands of, our unconquerable
Emperor Leopold at the time
of the coronation of the
Roman King.
I=L: the second work of this
same style under the title
"Second Selection or
Florilegium secundum"
F: under the title *Suavioris
Harmoniæ Instrumentalis
Florilegium Secundum*
F: second collection

In this *Florilegio Secundo* you can hope to find   I: second selection
my newly composed pieces which have eminently   I: *Arie di Balletti*
entertained distinguished guests in Passau,   F: and played with happy
and are nonetheless also suited to the   success
ballet practice of the children of the higher nobility;   F: of my compositions for
while in the meantime another work   the same instruments as
of instrumental music in an unusual   these
but elevated style is   F: a less known F: more
already sweating under   elevated style I: still more
the press at Passau.   elevated style along with
                                                           other titles will be printed in
                                                           Passau

Chapter 3

Texts from
Florilegium Secundum,
1698

[TITLE PAGE]

Suavioris Harmoniæ
INSTRUMENTALIS HYPORCHEMATICÆ
FLORILEGIUM SECUNDUM

Second Bouquet of
lovely instrumental
harmony

Second bouquet of lovely ballet pieces,

F: of ballet pieces of
a sweet instrumental
harmony for the
violins. L+ for the
dance.

consisting of sixty-two pieces, modelled

L: carefully crafted
"modulations"

on the current Ballet style and divided

F=I: the style which
is beginning more
and more to blossom
L: after the most
recent, and so the
most blossoming
dance style

into seven different keys and Partitas,
most diligently arranged and suitable for

I: bouquets or Partitas
in various keys
F: corresponding to
the bouquets

four or five strings together with a *Basso*

G: Geigen F: violons
I: stringed
instruments
F: + successfully

continuo if you wish, composed by Georg Muffat, Tutor to
His Esteemed Grace the Bishop of Passau's choir boys and
pages. These pieces were favorably performed with full
harmony for the

F: with full forces
L: with full choir

entertainment of
distinguished guests at

L: attendance
I: + princes and other

certain celebrations of the most esteemed Court of Passau,   L: + festive
as well as for the dancing practice of the noble youth. They
are enriched and augmented by a Foreword containing   L: studiously illustrated
certain important remarks translated into four languages, so
that one may better understand and become more easily
accustomed to the true and graceful manner of performing   F: method
                                                                          G: *expremieren*
these Ballets more exactly, and may obtain greater mastery   F: Airs
in this style of the noble art of music.   F: harmony

Available in Passau from the author. Printed by Georg
Adam Höller, 1698.

**[Note concerning the Four-Language
Introductory Materials]**

The title, dedication and Foreword of this work, together
with the useful remarks and explanations of the most
important points which are contained therein, can be
found in German in the violin part, in Italian in the *violetta*   F: *dessous*, or violin
part, and in French in the *violone* part, just as you find it   F: + *Haute-Contre* or
here in Latin [sic]. The examples cited in the above-
mentioned remarks, which should always be consulted with
the text, can be seen for the sake of convenience at the
beginning of each part-book in one of the four languages, in
alphabetical order as cited.

[Dedication]

To the most Venerable, Illustrious and Noble Lord,
JOHANN TRAUGOTT, Count of the Holy Roman Empire
and Lord of Kufstein, Canon and Chapter Member of the
Archdiocese of Passau, as well as to the Illustrious and
Noble Lord, LIEBGOTT, Count of the Holy Roman
Empire and Lord of Kufstein, Baron of Greillenstein, Lord
of Spitz, Weidenholtz, Hortheimb and Schwertberg, etc.,
Treasurer to His Imperial Roman Majesty; Silver-Treasurer
and Chief Administrator of both Archdioceses of Austria,
above and below the Enns River; Privy Councillor and Lord
Chamberlain, etc., to His Esteemed Grace of Passau.

Both Brother Lords, My Gracious Lords,
Most Venerable, Illustrious, and Noble   L: Most Venerable
Canon as well as   and Illustrious Lord
                                                                          Kanonikus

Illustrious and Noble
Marshal, Both Counts of the Holy Roman Empire,
Gracious Lords:

> L: Most Illustrious
> I: Illustrious Lords and my most honored employers.
> L: + and most well-meaning patrons
> L: of my instrumental dances in lovely harmony
> I: of a spirited and singing style
> L: + dared

In order that this second bouquet of my lovely ballet pieces, a work (as I hope) not unpleasant to the true

connoisseur of charming music,[1] may appear the more worthy of notice,
I have dutifully dedicated it to Your Esteemed Graces. And this is not without reason; for if in the most noble art of music the harmony is a
pleasant concordance of its tones, and if its happy resounding is brought forth most lovingly

> I: + sweet
> I: perfect
> I: sweet
> L: its song
> I: a wonderful, pleasant concordance in spirit and intent

in the presence of a similar concordance, so in truth this musical work of mine comes to Your Graces not of my volition, but rather because it is rightfully yours. For when I consider your imposing heritage, and see both brothers who have sprung from most noble line, and because I consider the unification of higher virtues inborn in this same line to be more complete,[2] I see that our spiritual and material

> L: + German

conditions are enhanced by the great services of both brothers. As for that which most enhances our unity of purpose, Your Graces are so renowned for your equal devotion to God, your equal zeal for and loyalty to the Serene House of Austria, your equal devotion to our most Gracious Princes, for kindness to equals and inferiors, and for good will towards everyone, that all souls are drawn to yourselves. I am silent regarding the honor of your noble lineage, which is more evident through its own glory than it could become through my modest words.

> I: wherein is shown the respect and love of the Universe

   I will only mention the radiant and most eternally honorable star of this eminent house, most worthy of honor: the Lord Ludwig, Captain-General of glorious memory in Upper Austria under the Most Serene Emperor Ferdinand III, Your Graces' overlord, the very embodiment of all praise

> L: grandfather
> I: + Count of Kufstein, your *Gran Padre*

---

[1] The grammatical construction (*der wahren anmuthigen Music Liebhaber*) is ambiguous; "true" and "charming" could apply either to "connoisseur" or to "music."

[2] Muffat's use of the words *Geblüte* and *reifer* in this passage invokes botanical imagery.

and heroism, who, to the most joyful relief of the whole
Imperial Court and Holy Roman Empire, administered a
difficult diplomatic mission to the Ottoman harbors, and
who, although entombed, lives in undying fame.

Because I am a musician and publisher of musical works,
there is one thing I cannot ignore: to wit, Your Esteemed
Graces' great and unusual appreciation and support (among
other tokens of your high regard) of music and of musicians.
Indeed, Your Esteemed Graces not only render all grace to
the connoisseurs of this noble art, but in this splendid
practice, as glorious as it is entertaining, you also grant
yourselves a few hours liberated from higher worries. It is a
noble activity of the spirit, to drive away all sluggishness of   L: + and of the spirit
the mind! Indeed, it is a pleasant refreshment following   I: pleasant refreshment of a
weighty duties.   generous spirit following
                                                                              serious worries.

   It is neither accidental nor a misjudgment   L: occupation for a
that these musical works of mine are dedicated   weakened spirit after heavy
to Your Graces, because some of these pieces were   work and exertion
composed by me at Your Esteemed Graces' most
gracious command, and resounded with festive
jubilation at many receptions for those pleasant and
benevolent guests of the esteemed House of Kufstein,
progenitors of the gracious   G: *Primitien*
Count Traugott.   I: Canon
   These pieces, as well as the others contained in this work   I: *Partite*
which were newly composed by me for the solemn
welcome of the princes and other distinguished persons   I: + in this house
(and nonetheless for the dancing practice of the noble
youth, through the sensible direction of all matters by His   L: leading
Grace the Lord Chamberlain), have brought such honor
upon themselves that through the perfect order of the
drama, the meaningful choreography of the dance, the skill   I: + and the scenes
of the dancing, and the impressive harmony of so many   I: + through the correctness
instruments, they have had on every occasion a favorable   of the harmony
and pleasant reception. Your Graces have shown me the   I: omit "impressive"
same good will, although I am not worthy of such
graciousness, and have also freed and protected me, through
your enduring power, from the treachery and persecution of   I: authority
the jealous. If there is something good, useful or
entertaining to be found in this Bouquet, then the
connoisseurs owe it to Your Graces, because among the
many proofs of your favor, your generosity has contributed
to the increased support of this work, including the
necessary printing expenses, without which not only my   I: + benevolently
works but also the outstanding works of other most excellent

men would remain buried in obscurity. It is certainly no small sign of generosity to help the arts through liberal charity, and to introduce them to others, for these are generally bare of wealth, and possessed only of knowledge.

May Your Graces deign to look upon this work of mine with favorable eyes, and to continue to hold me and my own under your protection. May you live for the everlasting increase and ornament of God, the Church, of the court, of the esteemed House of Kufstein, and at times also of music, which turns to you for help.

This I wish for Your Esteemed Graces,

Your obedient servant,

Georg Muffat.

I: + and scholars
I=L: Muses

I: virtue
I: this work of my poor talent
I: omit "and my own"
I: + and fame
I: + and to the brilliance

I: + with the lively eagerness of gratitude, a long series of happy years, with deepest bow

Foreword

I have noted, kind Reader, that my first Bouquet of lovely
ballet pieces, which were printed in Augsburg and which I
published at the beginning of the year 1695 as a precursor to
many future musical works to follow, has been favorably
received by many, especially by those connoisseurs who
greatly treasure an unaffected style, for whose entertainment
it was mostly intended. Moreover, I have noted that these
connoisseurs have

a great desire for the other Ballets which I promised would
come later. Therefore,
I consider it a good thing to present this
second Bouquet, larger by many pieces, for the worthy
entertainment of your souls and for your generous
consideration; it is more lively than the first because of
various musical devices, and hopefully more valuable
because of the usefulness of the appended remarks. It
contains no small number of those Ballets newly composed

by me in Passau, and which were heard with approval in
this esteemed Court both at the dance and when played on
several instruments. It owes its origin as much to
His Esteemed Grace's forceful zeal for the training of the
noble youth of the royal household, as to my desire to please
the ear, although they have also served various other
purposes, such as chamber music, table music, and night
music.
 As His Esteemed Grace took it upon himself to discover
what his esteemed and noble nephews, as well as his pages,
had learned in their studies and noble exercises, and in the
dance as well, Mr. Christian Leopold Krünner, appointed
chamber servant and meritorious Court Dance-Master to
His Esteemed Grace, sought me out to compose totally new
Arias utilizing certain useful ideas he had conceived, Arias
which could be danced to in costume and which could
utilize theatrical effects in order to be more impressive.

When I yielded up my meager
talents to this desire, His Esteemed Grace
looked on our work with such gracious eyes

F: flowing and natural style
I: an unaffected and singing style
L: flowing manner
F: to soon see other products of my small talent
F: my duty
L: just as the first

L: entertaining
L: as I hope

F: It contains a good many new pieces, which I composed in Passau and which were played and danced there with sufficient approval
L: . . . approved in this esteemed . . .

L: attention

L: at the same time
I: omit "chamber servant"
L: adapt

F=I=L: appearing in humorous costume and assisted by some theatrical devices
L: thus to be better
F: + collective

that he commanded us to prepare further dance exercises in this manner,

and to perform them for princely visitors and other prominent persons; and whenever they were performed, he was graciously pleased.

I wished to make this clear to you at the outset, kind Reader, so that if your ears find in these pieces something too coarse or unusual, you will not ascribe it to a dry or rough style; but rather, that you understand the necessity of the natural presentation belonging to the dance, which you can see explained on the carefully engraved plates in the *Basso continuo* and *Violino* parts.

Although I do not wish to be counted among those who take up every passing notion, for whom the most absurd ideas are the most highly prized, and of whom the words of Horace are true:

> *Nimium patienter utrumque*
> *Ne dicam stulte mirati,*

it nevertheless happens sometimes that one must occasionally yield a bit to better explain certain words, manners or gestures. I have therefore

taken great pains, since one must take great care to avoid all excesses, to soften the things that seem unusual in the upper part, namely the violin, with the grace of pleasant consonances, as well as to improve by artful scoring the all-too-ordinary passages in the middle and the bass parts.

Attached to this second Bouquet, you have some important remarks, as promised, which I have written as instructions for the proper playing of Ballets such as these, according to the opinions of the late Mr. Jean-Baptiste de Lully, which remarks are dedicated to your eagerness to know, which is not yet sufficiently instructed in this style to know of what it mainly consists, or how it differs from other ways and views. All of this will be brought out forthwith according to my meager ability: but I would also like to acknowledge, by the way, that someone who is a professional violinist, and well acquainted with the described manner (and there are already many of them in these lands), could have done this much better than I.

Marginal notes:

F=I: to prove our meager talents, each according to his profession, with dance exercises
L: publicly
L: in a spectacle

F: + fine

F: + the titles of the pieces in

F: *dessus*
L: + as ever
L: gulp down
L: influence
F: who consider the greatest madness to be a work of art

F: *on se peut permettre quelque chose en faveur d'une Imitation*
L: express

F: less natural
I: hard

F: Airs
F: the taste

L: type of method

Furthermore I assert that what I now say takes nothing away from the honest, deserved fame of many other famous violinists (whose flourishing number in Germany I myself consider estimable); they are to be considered no less worthy if they are not accustomed to this new manner, because of their other and higher share in this art.
If they were to add the lively, graceful Lullian charm to the musical confidence, agility of the hands, and multitude of

L: bind
I: if they play all that lies before them with musical surety and perfection
L: + as well

virtuosic effects over which they already possess mastery, they would not only equal the foreigners, but would easily surpass them.

F: the pleasant liveliness of the school of Mr. Baptiste de Lully
L: compositions

   Furthermore, I wish to refer you to an index of my already-published works, as well as forthcoming ones — the Partitas, their keys, and the years in which they were performed. I have appended it to the end of this work, to which I want to have referred you so that if you should hear something similar to my ideas in other places, you can tell from the chronology that I have not borrowed them, and

F=L: works

L: they have not become a fabrication

also so that, in recognition of what I hope to accomplish for your entertainment and further musical benefit, you will accept this my endeavor all the more benevolently.
Farewell.

F: + these labors and toils
F: that upon which I work
L: + and be kind

First Remarks

The Performance of the Ballets in the Lullian-French Manner,

for which the examples can be found in

order at the beginning of the Viola part.

This is how to play the Ballets on

violins in the manner of the most famous

Jean-Baptiste de Lully (which we here will understand in all its purity, and which is admired and praised by the most accomplished musicians of the world), a manner so sensible that one might scarcely think of anything more graceful or beautiful.

You should know, well-meaning connoisseur, so that I may reveal to you its most important secrets, that this manner has two characteristics: namely, that it focuses on what is most pleasing to the ear, and that it indicates the meter of the dance so exactly that one can immediately recognise the type of piece, and can feel the impulse to dance in one's heart and feet at the same time, contrary to all assumptions. In my opinion, there are five important rules which apply to this. First, that one stop the strings properly, for purity of intonation.
Second, the bow is to be drawn in the same way by all the

players. Third, one must always be aware of the true tempo, or the time and measure, appropriate to each piece. Fourth, one must pay close attention to the usual repetition signs that are written in, then to the characteristics of the style, and the art of dancing. Last, one should sensibly use various graces which make the ballet pieces much more beautiful and more charming, and which also brighten

---

F=I: of the author

F: On the manner of playing the *Airs de Balets à la Françoise* after the method of the late Mr. Lully.

F: + , to which one should refer from time to time, F: + together with that which will be said in this treatise
F: middle part, called *Viola*
I: French *Taille*
F: the manner
L: enliven
F: *airs de Balets*
F: *violons*
L: strings
F: according to the genius
F: + late

F: Europe
F: excellent
L: could
F: more exact, beautiful or pleasant
I: + in a few words

F: *mouvemens de la danse*

F: exact fingering
L: grip the strings rigorously and exactly
F: *vrai mouvement*
I: tempo or movement
F: + and the rendering of certain notes
I: + of certain notes and . . .
F: beautiful mannerisms and appropriate embellishments

them as if with sparkling gems. The following couplet applies to these:

Contactus, Plectrum, Tempus, Mos, atque Venustas
Efficient alacrem, dulcisonamque chelyn.

Fingering, Bowing, Tempo, Style, and Charm
Make the violin lively and lovely-sounding.

I. Contactus. On the Placement of the Fingers on the Violin

In the matter of how to stop the strings precisely to produce pure tones, there is no difference between the good players of any nation or manner of music, though they differ in nationality and type of music; only the weak students or clumsy bunglers in any place habitually make mistakes,

contrary to the custom of the masters. To learn to avoid wrong notes, there is nothing better than the constant instruction and correction of an experienced master, whom one expects to have already learned the fundamentals of violin playing (of which it is not our intention to speak here). I will only say the following: that to become accustomed to good intonation and to achieve and maintain a sensitive ear, one should undertake comprehensive training under a good master gifted with exceptionally good sense, and to practice with another connoisseur. One should avoid those teachers whose work brings the ears and the fingers more to ruin than to perfection. I have noticed that the mistakes most often made by those who are still inexperienced, and who finger the strings improperly, are these: that when two pitches lie a half-step apart (such as *mi* and *fa*, a and b♭, b and c, or also f♯ and g, c♯ and d, g♯ and a, etc.), that the lower pitch (*mi* or ♯) is not played high enough, and the upper pitch (*fa*) is not played low enough. And there is no lack of those who make the mistake of not applying the correct accidentals to trills or other graces, contrary to the proper distribution of the notes, the character of the musical style, or the harmonic relation to what has come before or what comes after. Last, the ear will be offended whenever the string is not pressed firmly enough to the fingerboard, as a nasty scraping sound will result.

I: + appropriate ornaments

F: these five points

I: + exact
F: On exact fingering.

L: string-players of Europe

L: + in the world
F: + unlearned and
L: + and precepts

F: taste

L: + who are wasted in the art and
I: omit "and the fingers"
I: omit "who . . . inexperienced"

F=I=L: + or ♭ *mol*

F: omit "or other graces"
F: proportions
F=I: the course of the notes or styles
F: + and punctually
F: + whistle and . . .
I: nasty, hideous, scraping hiss
L: + or whisper

II. *Plectrum.* The Use of the Bow

Text	Notes
	L: On the bow
Most Germans agree	F: German violinists
with the Lullists on the holding of the bow for the	F: French
violins and violas; that is, pressing the thumb against the	G: small and middle-sized violins
	F: top and middle parts
hair and laying the other fingers on the back of the bow. It is	I: *violoncino*
also generally held in this way for the bass by the Lullists;	F: French
they differ from the Italian practice, which concerns the	F: the top parts
small violins, in which the hair is untouched, and from that	I: soprano parts
of the bass gambists and others, in which the fingers lie	
between the wood and the hair.	
Although good violinists hold that the longer, steadier,	F: the best masters of all nations agree
more even, and sweeter the bow-strokes, the better, yet it has	
been observed that the Germans and the Italians do not	F: only rarely or accidentally with the French
agree with the Lullists, nor even to any great extent among	
themselves, in the matter of the rules for up- and down-	
bows. But it is well known that the Lullists, whom the	F: French
English, Dutch, and many others are already imitating, all	I: those who play like the late Mr. Baptiste, that is, the French, the English, the Dutch and Flemish, and many others
bow the most important notes of the musical meter,	
	L: in which the measure is given
	F: + most
especially those which begin the measure and which end a	
	F: persons of quality
cadence, and thus strongly show the motion of the dance, in	G: Cavaliers
the same way, even if a thousand of them were to play	F: of indicating the cadence so well
together. Thus when noble men returned to our lands from	I=L: so useful to the movement of the dance
	F: + often
these places, and did not find this unanimity among our	F: and bemoaned the distortions that resulted in the dance
German violinists, who were otherwise excellent, they	
noticed the difference in the concord of sound	
	F: + for the curious
and were amazed, and complained not infrequently about	F=I: the most important rules of bowing in the French manner
the improper movement of the dances. To help dispel this	
disorder and this danger of confusion,	L: certain rules for the connoisseur concerning bowing
I thought it wise to put forward here	
the most important rules concerning the bow. In the	

examples to be found at the beginning of the part marked
Viola, the sign (⊓) indicates down-bow, whereas (v) indicates
up-bow.

    1. The first note of a measure which begins without a rest,
whatever its value,

should always be played down-bow. This is the most
important and nearly indispensable general rule of the
Lullists, upon which the entire style depends, as well as the
main difference that distinguishes it from the other styles,
and upon which the other rules depend. The following
rules will show how the other notes are to be played in order
to conform to this rule.

    2. Of the notes which divide the beat into an even
number of parts in common time, which the theorists call
tempus imperfectum, all those which are odd-numbered
should be played down-bow, while those which are even-
numbered should be played up-bow. Odd numbers are 1, 3,
5, 7, 9, 11, etc. Even numbers are 2, 4, 6, 8, 10, 12, etc.

F: middle part, called viola
L: pull

L: of the meter as well as the
tempo
G: + or *Suspir,*
I: omit "whatever its value"
L: + strongly

F: secret of the bow
L: + of the bow
I: upon which the secret of
bowing depends and which
the other (rules) obey
L: . . . on which the other
rules seem to depend, like
students
G: *ordinari tempo oder Takt*

This rule also applies to the diminishing notes in triple time
and other meters. Diminishing notes are what I call notes
which are smaller than a beat.

F: + same

G: faster than those indicated
by the time signature
F: the beat

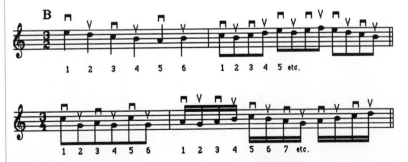

Rests which have the same values as the notes must also be   G: + and *Suspiria*
counted just as the notes are.

Most good violinists readily agree with   F: all the best masters
the Lullists in this rule.   F: second

3. Of the three notes which make up a whole measure in
triple time, the first would be played down-bow, the second
up-bow, and the third down-bow, when played slowly,   I: at least
according to Rule 1; this means one would play two down-
bows in a row at the beginning of the following measure.

If one plays faster, the second and third notes are often both   F: + in which the stroke,
played up-bow, the bow springing equally on each note.   called *craquer*, is divided
                                                                 exactly into two parts and
                                                                 should be executed with
                                                                 great lightness
                                                                 I: whereby the stroke is
                                                                 separated into two parts, and
                                                                 is to be performed most
                                                                 lightly in faster pieces
                                                                 L: with which it is lighter

4. A measure in six is divided in two,

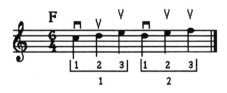

in nine it is divided in three,

and in twelve it is divided in four,

and each of the notes indicated in the time signature is
divided into three equal parts. The Lullists nearly always
play the first of these three equal notes down-bow, even if it
does not begin a measure, and the other two as a double up-
bow. When the first note follows a rest of equal value, it
must unquestionably be played down-bow, in triple time

F: measure
I: omit "The Lullists"
I: omit this sentence

G: *Suspir*

as well as in other compound meters.

5. If several notes follow one another, each of which
comprises a whole measure, each one must be played down-
bow.

L: is played as a "pull"

However, if several notes stand together in compound
meters of six or twelve, each of which comprises a complete
beat-unit of the measure, then they have even and odd
numbers, and thus are played with alternating up- and
down-bows according to Rule 2.

L: follow one another

In nine, they follow the first case under Rule 3.

I: + , which concerns triple time

6. Syncopated equal notes must also be played with alternating up- and down-bows.

F=L: which follow one another
L: now up, now down

This applies to equal notes.

7. As for unequal notes, the first of the smaller notes which follow the larger ones is considered odd-numbered, and one plays them either according to the rule,

I: + down

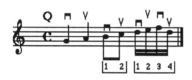

or, if the situation demands, with repeated down-bows,

L: as good judgment

or the two small notes are played with double up-bows, and the following notes are played immediately with alternating bowings.

Rests are counted exactly like notes of the same value for this rule.

L: + , however,
G: + or *Suspir*

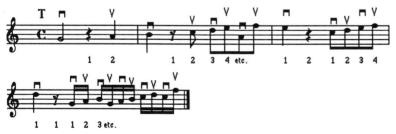

8. When three notes in compound time comprise a complete beat-unit, and the first is dotted, it is generally played down-bow.

9. If a measure, or a beat-unit, begins with a rest, and if the many successive notes which follow the rests complete either the measure or the beat-unit, the notes may be played with alternating up- and down-bows.

G: + or *Suspir*

10. If a small note is placed before the beginning of the measure,

or a fast passing note exists after a dot or breath,

or if a smaller note follows a larger syncopated one,

they must always be played up-bow. In this case the stroke is performed in two parts, if the previous note is also played up-bow.

F: + , to return to the lower half for the next note

In Courantes, those notes which begin even-numbered measures (for example, the second, fourth, sixth, or other even-numbered measures, if one reckons them in triple time) are occasionally exempted from Rule 1 because of the fast tempo. These may sometimes be played up-bow with better facility and disposition of the bow than the other way, taking a liberty with Rule 1, if one always plays those notes which begin odd-numbered measures, and thus more strongly show the dance rhythm, down-bow. In the next three examples, I have marked the liberties from the rules with a *.

F: disposition and ease

F: most

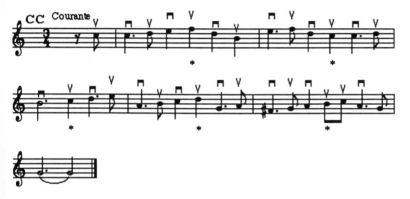

That is why in dances called Courantes, not one, but two measures are shown together. Further, if only the most important rule, the one concerning the first note of the measure, is obeyed, one must often disobey the other rules (the fourth, eighth, and tenth rules, those concerning the beginning of a measure unit and the treatment of the remaining small notes), in compound meters, due to the speed of Gigues, Canaries, and similar pieces. One can learn how to proceed with these multiply combined points in Example DD.

F: omit sentence

The same is true in Bourées and similar pieces, due to their speed; in order to uphold Rule 1, the other notes which follow may be played contrary to Rule 7, as shown in Example EE.

F=I: + which often repudiates the eighth rule
F: by upholding Rule I, one bows according to Example EE without hesitation

Finally, when two eighth or sixteenth notes are paired as a grace, they can either be played separately,

F: + of another note

or (which is more lovely) played together with one bow, as it seems appropriate.

F: slurred
F: the previous notes with
F=I: + or two

   Those who indiscriminately play the first note of a measure up-bow (as often happens among the Germans and Italians in triple time, especially if the first note is shorter than those following) are in direct conflict with the Lullian way of playing. This opposite view and this transgression of the most important Lullian rule results in a great difference

F: omit "Lullian"
F=I: the above-noted first
F=I: this great difference in bowing
F=L: those which depend on the first note

in the sound, both in the first notes and in those which follow. To better explain this difference, I have set down some notes in Example HH as they would be bowed in certain German or Italian ways of playing, as opposed to the Lullian way shown below.

F=I: omit "as . . . Lullian"

When one slurs the short note after a dot to the note which follows, breaking

Rule 10 as shown in Example LL, this contradicts the liveliness of the music.

The Lullian manner can be seen in Example MM.

On the other hand, it is permitted by the Lullists, as the

need arises, to take the aforementioned note in the same bow as the previous note.

These are the most important rules of bowing among the Lullists, which apply exactly and uniformly to the violin as well as the viola and the bass. The greatest skill of the

Lullists lies in the fact that even with so many repeated down-bows, nothing unpleasant is heard, but rather that they wondrously combine a long line with practiced dexterity, a variety of dance movements with the exact uniformity of the harmony,

and lively playing with an extraordinarily delicate beauty.

F: + with one bow
G: *Fuselle*
I: + or a small breath
L: small note
F=I: Rule 7 [sic]
I: the liveliness of the Lullists

F: One plays in French as in Example MM

F: if it should occur, it is permitted
F: little note
I: + , which is separate,
L: small note

F: omit "exactly and uniformly"
F: top part
F: *parties du milieu*
F: + true
F: that the length of the lines is wonderfully bound up with a marvelous liveliness, an astonishing uniformity of beat with the variety of movements, and a sensitive beauty with lively playing
L: the liveliness of the sounds

III. *Tempus*. On the Beat, or Tempo

There are three things that are important to consider about musical time.

First, that one knows well the tempo ascribed to each piece. Second, that one holds to that tempo with constant steadiness for as long as the piece is played, becoming neither slower nor faster. Third, that one somewhat alters and accommodates the values of certain notes for greater grace.

1. The first point concerns the knowledge of which mensural signs and pieces should be played slowly and which quickly; I have discussed this in the Foreword of my first *Florilegium* (which was printed in Augsburg in 1695), to which, in short, I refer the benevolent Reader. He can find my first Ballet work for sale in that same city at the shop of Wilhelm Pannecker.

Later I will undertake to explain why the Lullists use the sign 2 or the half-circle with a stroke through it, called *Alla breve*, in their Ballets. To become acquainted with the proper tempo of the Ballets,

what helps the most, other than regular practice with the Lullists, is an understanding of the art of the dance, in which most Lullists are well versed. That is why one should

not be amazed at their exact observance of that tempo.

2. Not everyone can hold a set beginning tempo with constant steadiness for as long as a piece is played, and many fail to do so in part or in whole. One errs in whole when one plays a piece either more slowly or more quickly than its nature and attributes demand; but one errs in part

when one measure is played faster than the others, or when one note is played faster or slower than its value demands.

To avoid the errors which violate these two rules, one must first reject the abuse being spread by many, in which every piece, indiscriminately, is performed slowly the first time, faster the second time, and quite rushed the third

---

F: omit "On . . . Tempo"
L: On the time

F: about the movement of the beat
F: *mouvement*
L: true tempo which belongs to

F: beauty

L: + more

F: + or collection of my Ballet airs
F: the first of my works for the violins
F: another time
L: are more frequently called *Alla breve* than our four-beat *tempo ordinario*, which is indicated by a simple half-circle
F: more often used than the normal ones in four
F: + I find that
F: in each piece
F: the best violinists in France
I: French players
F=L: be amazed that they find the tempo so well and know how to hold to it

F: slower
L: too slowly
L: too quickly
L: manner
F: omit "than . . . demand"
F: slower or
F: omit "than . . . demands"

F: + very
F: faster and
F=L: very fast and rushed

time. Second, one must take care not to linger in cadences a
longer or shorter time than the notes stipulate. Third, one
must not play the last measure faster than the first, but rather   F: on the contrary
always adhere more to moderation than to haste. Fourth,
one must not be alarmed by sixteenth notes, and thus run
ahead all too much, but rather, "make haste slowly." Fifth,   F: play with moderation and
in triple time one must give the third and last beat its proper   precision
value, which many play imperceptibly shorter than its due,   F: unnoticeably
and thus rush the beat and make it uneven. I have marked   F: omit "and . . . uneven"
these notes with a * in Example OO.

The error to be avoided in this sixth point is that in the
second and fourth quarter notes, when the marking is 2 or   G: *Fusellen*
Alla breve (especially in Gavottes), and the even-numbered
beats in common time (**c**), run ahead; these are marked
with a * in Example PP.

They should be rather more held back than rushed.   F: + instead
   3. Diminishing notes of the first order, which in common   I: in *Tempus ordinarius*
time (**c**) are a series of sixteenth notes,   *imperfectus*
                                                                       L: four-beat *Imperfectum*
                                                                       F: + in duple time or *Alla*
                                                                       breve are crochues,
                                                                       I: + which in *Alla Breve*
                                                                       tempo are eighths,
                                                                       L: + in duple time or *Alla*
                                                                       breve are simple *Fusen,*
and in lively triple meters and moderate compound meters   F: faster
are those notes which are half as small as a beat, are not   I: twice as fast

bowed by the Lullists just as they are (which is dull, crude, and unlovely to hear),

G: *gestrichen*
L: performed
F: omit "by the Lullists"
L: seems
L: uncultivated, boring

but a bit altered, as if all the odd-numbered notes were given a dot; therefore the following notes would be played faster. Example QQ shows the various types of rhythms, while Example RR shows how the more noble altered notes are played, if the tempo permits.

F: + *à la Françoise*
F: + since they are longer,
F: in various meters
F: in what manner one
expresses them

IV. *Mos.* More on the Lullists' Practices That Serve Our Purpose

L: + customs and . . .

1. The instruments should be tuned exactly to each other, before the arrival of the audience if time permits, or, at least, as quietly and quickly as possible.
2. One should refrain from making any noise, and from warming up in too chaotic a manner. If one fills the air and

F: + before the beginning of
the performance

the ears with this sort of thing before the Symphony, the distaste which results will nearly overshadow the pleasure which follows.

    3. The pitch to which the Lullists tune their instruments is generally a whole-step lower, and in theatrical productions even one-and-a-half steps lower, than our German pitch. The so-called *Cornetton* seems to them to be

quite too forced and piercing. If it were up to me, I would

select the so-called choral pitch because of its liveliness combined with sweetness, with less powerful strings than the others.

    4. The parts should be judiciously distributed and apportioned according to the number of musicians, so that one can distinguish and perceive everything well and beautifully. And all the best players should not be assigned to the first violin (or upper) part, so that the middle voices seem robbed of the

necessary players; this manner of harmony, whose grace is concealed in the lower parts, would be deprived. It is most regrettable that this often happens

because of the ambition of certain tactless people to play the first part.

    5. As for the instruments, a somewhat more narrowly-made viola

would serve better for the *Violetta* part, which the French call *haute contre*,

than a violin or small violin.

L: a disgust will thereby be created which will surely be greater than the following pleasure
F: French
F: Operas
F: a minor third
I: + *Cornetto*, which they call cornetto pitch
L: the pitch called cornetto pitch
F: + too high,
L: + sharp,
L: noisy
F: the first pitch, which the Germans call "old choral pitch,"
I: the so-called "old choral pitch," which is a whole-step lower
F: + double-
L: duplicated

F=I=L: + the usual graces
F: upper part
F: + and the bass
L: + or the lower voices
L: + and appropriate
F: whereby the greatest grace which is concealed in them
L: this harmony, whose grace this style conceals in the lower parts
F: the stupid ambition to be the first which gets into some people's heads
F: *Viol du milieu*, smaller-made than the *Taille*
L: middle viola
I: sound
F: + *haute-contre*, in Italian
F=I: omit "which . . . contre"
I: + more
G: *kleine Geige*
F: *dessus de Violon*
L: small high-violin

The bass part is given of necessity to the small bass violin, which the Italians call *violoncino* and the Germans call the French bass.

It does not seem possible to dispense with this instrument without thereby distorting the proportions of the harmony. The director should decide whether or not to add more players to the part. If there are a sufficient number of musicians,

the large bass, which the Germans call *Violone* and the

Italians call *Contra Basso*, will bring out a special majesty, albeit one of which the Lullists have not yet made use in the Ballets.

6. I have described what must be noted about repeats in the Foreword of my first *Florilegium*, which the well-meaning connoisseur can examine. The other things, with a little practice, can be easily grasped from the words which appear in the parts, as well as repeat signs and final signs marked with the word *Fin* (if one is to stop in the middle).

7. Finally, it will greatly help to keep the tempo steady if each violinist, like the Lullists, marks the tempo with an appropriate motion of the foot.

V. *Venustas*. On Graceful Ornamentation

   Those who unreasonably hold forth that the Lullian violin ornaments only

obscure the melody or are composed only of trills, have not properly considered the matter, or have never adhered to the true Lullists,

F: *petite Basse à la Française*
I: *violoncino*
F=I: omit "which . . . bass"
F: + true

G: *Regenten*
L: + based on the number of musicians
F=I: one can double the number of players on the part, according to the size of the orchestra
I: large
F: + or Contra Bass, as the Italians call it
I: Contrabass or Great Violin, as the Italians call it
F=L: *violone*
F=I: omit "and . . . *Basso*"
F: French

F: or collection

F: + and signs
F: to the pieces

F: small
L: discrete

I: Ornamentation.
L: On beauty and ornaments.

G: *Geigenmanier*
I: the ornaments
F: who ascribe to the French ornamentation without restraint
F=I: + and harmony
L: + or the tune
F: been a disciple of

but only to false ones. On the contrary, those who are immersed in the nature and variety, the beauty, the sublimity, and true origins of the proper use of the ornaments, which spring from the purest fountain of vocal technique, have to this day noticed nothing which hinders the distinction of the melody or the precision of the harmony. Indeed, they have discovered a profusion of attributes with which to decorate what is simple, to relieve what is rough, and everywhere to enliven what is dull with a wondrous liveliness. Although there is a greater number and variety of ornaments than many believe,

F: of imitators of the school of the late Mr. de Lully
I: of false students of the late Mr. Lully or only false imitators of this style

F: They have on the contrary discovered a profusion of things which are able to enrich, to sweeten, and through a wondrous liveliness to awaken, all things simple, raw, or dull which can be found in the first two voices.
I: . . . rather they have found, on the contrary, everything which can enrichen, sweeten, and enliven what sounds simple, raw, or dull in the two top parts of the music, with a wondrous form of life.

I will describe at this time only the most important and essential, and then

(God willing) I will speak more about this, as well as other things, elsewhere.

The mordant, or half trill (✷),
begins and ends on the principal note and trills to the note a half-step below, which is often therefore raised with a sharp (♯); it is often played very short, and often a single oscillation will suffice.

L: + perhaps
F: + briefly
F: one day
F: with God's help
F: will speak of it elsewhere
L: omit "or half trill"

L=G: *Semitremulus*
F: *Pincher*
I: *Pizziao*
F: or *Pincement ou Tremblement coupé*
I: or *Mordante*
G: or *Zwicker*
G=F=I=L: + or ✗

The *trill*, the true, old, and complete trill, begins on the

F: *tremblement ou fredon*
I: *trillo*
G=L: *Tremulus*
G=F=I=L: **t** etc.

note above the principal note and ends on the principal note. It is either *simple* (**tr**, **+**, **~**),

curved, in which it touches the lower note and

F: *Réfléchissant*
I: *Riflesso*
G=L: *Reflexus*
F: one single time
F: + a little

thereafter comes to rest on
the principal note,

or *confluent* (flowing together) (**t⌣**),

F: *Roulant*
I:+ , which is also called
Groppo
G=L: *Confluens*
F: + (the French call this an
agrément, a term they
employ a little too much)
F: + which accompany this
note. This is called *double
cadence* by harpsichordists

which is not so different from *curved* except that it does not come to rest on the principal note, but flows quickly to

the next note; it is often composed of two sixteenth notes put together.

Grace notes (♪) are notes placed before or after the principal note. There are six types of these, three before and three after the principal note.

G=F: *Accentuation*
I: *Accentuatione*
L: *Accentuatio*

Those which are placed before the principal note are (1) the *upper accent*, one

F: *Sur-accent*
I: *Pre-accento*
G=L: *Præaccentus*

note above, (2) the *lower accent*, one note

F: *Sub-accent*
I: *Sotto-accento*
G=L: *Subsumtio*

below, and (3) the *leap*, a pitch removed

F: *Sursaut*
I: *Salterello*
G=L: *Insultura*

from the principal note by a leap. Those which come after the principal note are
(4) the *superior* (generally called *Accent*), one note above,

F: a note a third above

F: *Superficie* or *Accent*
I: *Superficie* or *Accento*
G=L: *Accentus*

(5) the *relaxation*, one note down, and

F: *Relachement*
I: *Calamento*
G=L: *Remissio*

(6) the *dispersion*,

F: *Dispersion*
I: *Dispersione*
G=L: *Disjectio*

which once again is a leap.

F: the third or the other above

The *appoggiatura* (♪) is a grace note

G: *Adminiculation*, known by the Italians as *Appoggiatura*, called *Anlehnung* (/ or \),

as described above, and places on

I: from above, omit "known by the Italians"
L: from above, omit "known . . . *Anlehnung*"

the second of two notes a repetition of the previous pitch.

F: the *Port de voix*, consists of the first three types of grace notes

The *anticipation*, however, is placed

F: *Préoccupation*
I: *Preoccupatione*
G=L: *Préoccupation*
F: + which is like the last
three types of grace notes
G: second [sic] of two notes

on the first of two notes, and adds to the first note the pitch
of the second.

The *confluence* fluidly binds together two or more notes
in one bow. It is *simple* or *figured*; the *simple*, which is
notated (⌢ or ⌣) in the composition, includes no other
notes.

F: *coulement*
I: *Confluenza*
G=L: *Confluentia*
G: + the "flowing together"
or *Schleiffung*

The *figured* version includes other notes than those printed,
and is either *straight* or *curved*. The *straight figured*

F: *droit*
I: *dritta*
L: *recta*
G: *gerade*
L: flows
L: omit (. . .)
I: +, to which one jumps

confluence (⌢ or ⌣) proceeds stepwise (without leaps)

to the far note through the pitches which lie in between;

the *curved* one, however, (〰, 〰) loops back and forth.

F: *tournoyant*
I: *girellante* or *girevole*
L: *flexuosa*
G: *gebogene*
L: loops from here to there

The *exclamation* (⁎) is a type of *confluence* which ascends stepwise

through three pitches, and either arrives at the next note,

F: *Exclamation*
I: *Esclamazione*
G=L: *Exclamatio*
G: goes back to its note,

or arrives above the next note.

G: goes on further above its note.

The *turn* (∾) is another type of *confluence* in which three

pitches are, as it were, wrapped up in a circle, sometimes simple,

G: + or *Einwicklung*
F: + , which many call *agrément*
I: *Involtura*
L: *Involutio*
F: touches

but sometimes with a trill.

The *coruscation* (⸪) is distinguished from the [*figured*] *confluence* only in that the notes are played distinctly, and, so to speak, with a hopping bow-stroke.

F: *Petillement*
I: *Crocchiamente*
G=L: *Subcrepatio*

The *diminution* substitutes for the long notes many other small notes, which animate and suit the composition and are often played with separate bows.

I: *Diminutione* or *Passaggi*
G=L: *Diminutio*
F: each has its own bow-stroke

The *tirade* (⌇ or ⌇) runs stepwise with the greatest speed of the bow to its note.

F: + or *Course*
I: *Tirata* or *Corsa*
L: *Incursio*
G: *Incursion* or *Tirada*
F: + quickness and with . . .
L: quickly and with . . .

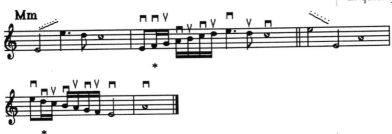

The *staccato* (·) is when each note is played as if it were followed by a rest.

F: *Détachement*
I: *Staccamento* or *Staccato*
G=L: *Disiunctio*
G=F=I=L: + (| or)
G: *Suspirs*

These twelve figures will be enough for now; we will, however, speak briefly about their use. Of the notes which occur in a composition, some are considered good and

F: + or ornaments

G: noble
F=L: good, noble, or principal
F: paltry or bad

some are considered bad. The good ones are those which naturally linger in the ear. Those are the longer ones, those which begin an essential part of the measure, or those which are dotted, as well as odd-numbered notes of smaller

L: + or seem
to radiate a
certain calm
F: + somewhat

values, which should be taken down-bow. The bad ones are

F: mostly
L: + tiny or

all the others, namely those which do not satisfy the ear so well, but rather inspire a desire to go further. See Example

L: + expectations of the
L: as well
F: + on each note

Oo, in which I have marked the good notes "g" and the bad notes "b". If these markings are observed, the following rules will be better understood.

G: n (Latin: *nobiles*)
G: v (Latin: *viles*)

1. *Mordants* are appropriate nearly everywhere, except on the very fastest of notes. Nor is it forbidden to play two or more in a row, if the notes are of only moderate speed.

F: if the speed is not too fast

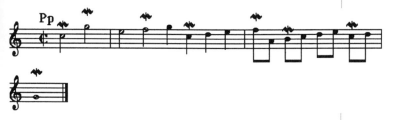

2. It is seldom good to begin a piece or a section, or an ascent or descent, with a *trill*, except on *mi* or ♯. In these cases (*mi* or ♯), however, the *simple trill* as well as the *curved trill* is often used.

L: the melody, sections
F: sharp

3. If one ascends by step,

the *appoggiatura* is added to the good notes, either by itself
(7) or with a *mordant* (8). If the notes are too fast, this
manner is saved for the slower good notes, when next they
come (9). Sometimes the *curved trill* is played on
slower ascending notes, either by itself (10) or prepared with
a *grace note* (11); the *appoggiatura* can also be gracefully
added (12), or a *confluent trill* can be used (13). To trill on
the good notes in an ascending passage sounds somewhat
harsh. But if it must be done, the trill should be softened
with the *anticipation* (14). Therefore *mi* and ♯ are excepted
from this rule, since they should nearly always be decorated
with a *trill*, whether they are good or bad notes, as long as
they do not ascend too rapidly (15).

F: ornament

F=I: + bad
L: + un-noble

    4. In descending passages with conjunct motion,

here and there the good notes, especially those with dots,
are played with very light and simple *trills* (16). Sometimes
the weak, descending slow notes are also most beautifully
played this way, by themselves (17) or with the anticipatory

L: some kind of simple

relaxation as well (18); rapid descending passages are played
with trills only here and there on certain good notes (19).
    5. In ascending leaps,

the *appoggiatura* is added to the good notes, either by itself
(20) or with a *mordant* (21). Sometimes the good notes are
played with a *straight confluence* to enliven the harmony,
either by itself (22), or (which is even more beautiful) mixed
with a *confluent trill* (23). The very liveliest is the *tirade*,
which can sometimes be used, but only with discretion (24).
An ascending leap of a third is best relieved by an ascending
exclamation (25), which is used by the Lullists only in this
place, and elsewhere hardly at all. While it is otherwise an
error to leap up to a *trill*, it is often permitted to do so to a
mi or ♯ (26).

F: + figure

F: sharp

    6. In descending disjunct passages,

trills are seldom employed, except when one leaps down a third (27), or leaps down to a *mi* or a ♯ (28), and in that case they should be mostly *simple* or *bent trills*. Further, a descending leap is most gracefully announced by an *anticipation* (29), a *confluence* (30), a *coruscation* (31), or in a lively way with a *tirade* (32). But the most lovely is a *confluence* with a delicate trill and an *anticipation* on the penultimate note of the descent (33).

    7. In cadences, certain notes require a *trill*, and certain notes reject a *trill*.

F: sharp

F=I: omit "and an
anticipation"

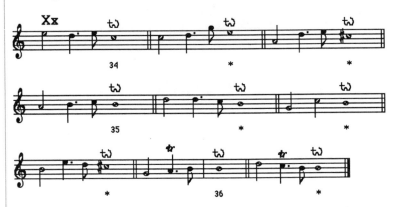

The notes which end cadences are seldom given a *trill*, unless one leaps down a third (34) or descends by step (35), or comes, with an *appoggiatura*, to a *mi* or ♯ (36).
I am attaching to the examples
six graceful cadential formulas in the Lullian manner, numbered 1, 2, 3, 4, 5, and 6, with which

I: omit "or descends . . .
appoggiatura"
F: sharp
F: omit "to the examples"
F: the most frequent and
most beautiful ways of
forming and decorating the
cadences in the good taste of
the Lullists
I: the six most delicate and
most often-used formulas
for . . .

you might note
the proper and reasonable use of the most important figures.

I: the good Reader
F=I: + which bejewel the
playing

8. Since *diminutions* invented on the spur of the moment can seldom be trusted, I have included some useful ones in Example Yy.

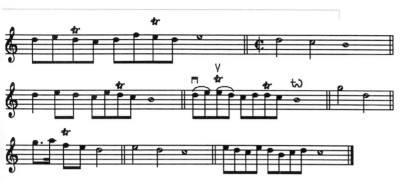

9. Two *trills* in a row are not considered good. They are, however, permitted

if a *grace note* is placed between them (37), or when the following note is a *mi* or ♯ (if a trill is added to the previous note according to the above-stated rule) (38).

10. Finally, the *staccato* can sometimes be used to evoke the movement of the dance with more animation,

L: + hard
F: + , which is harder (*plus dure*) than the previous

at least in notes of medium value (39), whole triple notes (40), or beat-units in compound time (41). But indeed, it must be done without affectation and without ripping at the

strings, but always with vigor, moderation, and purity.

F: measures

L: + and without being frivolous
L: elegance
F: always emphatically and without affectation or ripping (at the strings)

Thus I can rightly say that

F: I venture to say
L: I assure you, not immoderately

the entire Lullian manner of ornamentation is contained in the brief form of these ten rules, in which (along with what was indicated in the previous sections) are contained the greater part of the special beauty of this manner, its

freshness and grace, which can distinguish it from the other manners.
There are many different things which work against this

most noble element of music, which certain idle scoffers

consider useless:
namely Neglect, Impropriety, Excess, and Incompetence. Through Neglect,

the melody as well as the harmony becomes empty and unadorned; through Impropriety, it becomes hard and barbaric; through Excess, it becomes confused and ridiculous; and finally through Incompetence, it becomes awkward and self-conscious. It is therefore essential that one have such diligence in using these valuable musical graces (wherever they are appropriate), such care as to discern where they belong, and such agility as beautifully to express them, that the slightest omission of the *appoggiatura* in ascending passages, or of trills on *mi* or ♯ (at least on the good notes), as well as the slightest *trill* on a

leap, the slightest misuse of the *exclamation* elsewhere than learned, or the slightest difficulty in playing such figures quickly, fluently, and carefully, will soon betray those who are not sufficiently experienced in this style, but who have long imagined themselves to have ascended to the mountaintop of Lullian perfection. All these things will be discussed exactly, in more detail, in my (God willing) other *Florilegii*, which (God willing) will appear one by one.

And so, well-meaning Reader, may you think well of these first remarks of mine, held back until now, communicated to you and brought together with special care in this brief arrangement for your pleasure; and may you generously protect it, out of your natural taste for music, from all jealous people and interpreters who contradict my ideas. Should you find something defective in this work, attribute

---

Marginal notes:

G: *Manierwesen*
F: secret of the ornaments in French playing
L: + in the manner of a synopsis
F: + modest
F: of this manner
F: easily four
I: four
F: the most important part of the melody
I: most noble part of the melody
F: unimportant
G: *Unterlassung, Uneigenschaft, Überfluß und Untauglichkeit*

F: + the playing becomes

F: such circumspection

F: facility
L: integrity
F: sharp
F: omit "at least"
L: lightest
L: + upward
F: a dreary *exclamation*

F: with God's help
F: collections or *Florileges*
I: excerpts of Ballets
F: my dear Reader
L: well-meaning connoisseur
L: + made under your authority

it to my inability, and if you should find something good, attribute it to GOD the Almighty as giver of all grace, and pray to him to grant quiet times, favorable for the Muses, to his Christendom and especially to our Germany; and to grant me, as I wander Parnassus with my various troubles, unnoticed by all the envious, under the most serene shadow of the Austrian Eagle and the most gracious protection of the archiepiscopate of Passau and Lamberg, continued life and health, and to graciously supply me with such dispositions of temperament and of my affairs that I may better clarify these materials and complete more of the works I have in mind, out of my love for you.

F: + gifts and

F: + various paths of

L: of your grace

Index
of the Partitas
contained in this
second *Florilegio* or
Bouquet

	G: *Partien*
	I: work

First Partita in D, called *Nobilis Juventus,*

F=L: + natural
L: + *dictus*
L: omit "or Noble Youth"

or Noble Youth, in which material is taken from the manner and fashion of various peoples; composed and danced in the year 1691.

Second Partita in G, called *Laeta Poësis* or
Merry School of Poetry; prepared and performed in the year 1692.

G=F=I=L: +
L: + *nuncupatus*

Third Partita in A,

F=L: + natural
I: + called
L: + *intitulatus*

Illustres Primitiæ or
Esteemed Progenitors, which contains pieces in the most common dance forms;

L: forms
I: the most often-used dance pieces of the year 1693
L: dance art
L: prepared

composed and performed in the year 1693.

F=I: omit "composed . . . 1693."

Fourth Partita in D major,

F=I=L: + major third
G: + with ♯♯
L: + *vocatus*

Splendidæ Nuptiæ or Eminent Wedding, which saw the light of day in 1691.

Fifth Partita in G minor, *Colligati Montes* or Merged Mountains;

I=L: + minor third
L: + *appellatus*
G: + with ♭♭ *mol*
F=I: omit "resounded . . . in"

resounded with great harmony in 1692.

Sixth Partita in A major,

I=L: + major third
G: + with ♯♯
L: + *dictus*

named *Grati Hospites* or Welcome Guest;
performed in 1693.

Seventh Partita in E minor,

F=I=L=G: + with the minor third
L: + *nuncupatus*

Numæ Ancile or Shield of Heaven;
also composed and danced in 1693.

I: performed
L: sung and performed
F: omit "composed . . . in"

Eighth Partita in E or E-flat,

I: + and last
F=I=L=G: + with the major
third

called *Indissolubilis Amicitia,* or Inseparable Friendship;
performed as the Ballets in one of the theater pieces on

I: + if you wish
L: be it soft (moll = minor),
be it hard, with major third
L: + *intitulatus*

"The Friendship of Damon and Pithias," in 1695.

L: Story

Index
of the Author's Works
in Print

1. *Apparatus Musico-Organisticus*, most humbly dedicated to our unconquerable, all-gracious Emperor LEOPOLD the First, for the most glorious coronation of Her Majesty the Roman Empress and His Majesty the Roman Emperor. This great royal work, decoratively engraved in copper and published at great expense, was most humbly placed in the hands of His Serene Highness our Almighty Emperor by the author, was most graciously heard by His Imperial Majesty and was received with the richest gift of grace. It contains twelve pieces which the organists call *Toccatas*. Three other lively pieces are included, namely a *Ciacona*, a *Passacaglia*,

L: most unconquered
L: most glorious coronation of the spouse and the son

F: on princely paper
I: + 1690

I: *Toccatas*
F: Italians
I: omit "which . . . *Toccatas*"
I: omit "Three . . . pieces"

and a new Blacksmith Aria and its variations. The

F: *Cyclopejade* or an allusion to the hammer-wielding Cyclops and the hammer-blows of the blacksmith.
L: harmonious *Cyclopejade*
I: the keyboard art

connoisseur of this art will find therein abundant practice. This work is available from the author, from Georg Adam

L: It offers therein abundant practice of the organist's art
F: in Passau

Höller, Book-printer here, and also from Johann Baptist Mayr, Court and Academic Printer in Salzburg.

2. *Suavioris Harmoniæ Instrumentalis Hyporchematicæ FLORILEGIUM PRIMUM*, or First Bouquet of Lovely Ballet Pieces, which contains fifty pieces for four or five strings along with *Basso continuo* (if you wish), mostly arranged in the French manner. It was printed in Augsburg by Jakob Koppmayr in1695, and can be found at the shop of Wilhelm Pannecker, bookseller there.

L: omit "or . . . Pieces"
L: *modulationen* for the dance, commonly called "Balet"
G: *Geigen*

3. Then, in the present, this Second Bouquet of lovely Ballet Pieces. Among my other future works to be published, there will be more works in this same manner, with the titles *Suavioris Harmoniæ Instrumentalis FLORILEGIUM TERTIUM, QUARTUM, QUINTUM,* etc. (that is, Third, Fourth, Fifth, etc., Bouquet of lovely Ballet Pieces), including important attached remarks, which (God willing) will follow in proper order in their own time.

I: in the French style

L: the *Florilegien*
F: omit "*Suavioris* . . . willing"

May you then, kind Reader, benevolently accept this work of mine, until I give you in a few months that which I

F: my dear Reader
F: first work

promised a year ago in my first *Florilegium* or Bouquet, that
precious and nearly finished work, arranged in an unusual
manner: *Exquisitioris Harmoniæ Instrumentalis Gravi-
Jucundæ SELECTUS PRIMUS*, or First Collection of
Select Instrumental Music, both serious and light-hearted.
This work contains not only the pleasant, lively beauty of
the late Monsieur Baptiste de Lully, but also has the
Italian charm mixed in at the proper time, and includes as
well a Foreword containing a few reminders which concern
this manner.

F: omit "a year ago"

I: + Arias or Ballets of the

F: the heavy, sad Italian
passages
I: Italian pathos
I: in certain places
F: + the harmony

Farewell; and may you inspire me with your patronage to
additional works.

F=I: my Muse, through a
benevolent reception of my
meager production
L: my Muse
F: greater

Chapter 4

Texts from *Auserlesene Instrumentalmusik*, 1701

[TITLE PAGE]

EXQUISITIORIS HARMONIÆ
INSTRUMENTALIS GRAVI-
JUCUNDÆ SELECTUS PRIMUS

First Collection of Select Instrumental

Music, both serious and light-hearted, consisting of
twelve excellent concertos worked out with
great diligence for the special amusement of the ear in a
hitherto unusual manner. These works sound as well with
few players as with many;
that is, they are satisfying and graceful to perform with
five parts,

or with the three essential parts alone, along with the *Basso
continuo* if you wish,
but are much more substantial in, so to speak, two choirs, a
large one and a small one,

in order that the special distinctive characteristics might be
more clearly distinguished and that the harmony might be
more greatly emphasized. This work is not only quite
suitable for the entertainment of the connoisseur, the cheer
of social gatherings, and for dinner music and serenades, but
is also notable because of the many distinctive features of
the Arias, the result of new combinations of serious and
light-hearted ideas, indeed, of the unique alternations,

G: Auserlesene
Instrumentalmusik
F: instrumental harmony
L: heavy
L: songs
I: omit "with great diligence"
F: unique concertos in a new
style
L: + equally
F: *violons*
G: *Geigen*
F: only three *violons*
L: + if you wish
F: but with great splendor
L: excellent
F: omit "satisfying . . . speak"
I: *Concerto grosso*
I: *Concertino piccolo*
L: + in the music
F: omit "in order that . . ."
L: extremely
F=L: + of music
L: + most
L: modulations
F: mixtures
L: + soon

interruptions,
and skirmishes between
the full choir and the small solo trio.
It is no less useful because of the Foreword in four
languages, which describes
the manner in which to perform these concertos well.

From Georg Muffat, *Kapellmeister* to His Serene Eminence
the Cardinal of Lamberg, Bishop and Prince of Passau.
Printed in Passau by the widow Maria Margaretha Höllerin,
1701.

The titles, dedication, and very important Foreword on the
graceful performance of these concertos, along with the
table of contents and an index of the works of the author in
print, can be found in German in the *Violino primo
Concertino* part, in Italian in the *Violino secondo Concertino*
part, and finally in French in the *Violone, e Cembalo
Concerto grosso* part, just as you read them here in Latin
{sic}.

F: breaking off
F: battles
F: large
F: It also contains a
Foreword
L: method

L: + the author
F: *maître de Musique*

F: on the good playing

[Dedication]

Most Venerable, Illustrious and Noble Lord Maximilian
Ernst, Count of the Holy Roman Empire and Lord of
Scherffenberg, Esteemed Provost and Archipresbyter of the
Archdiocese of Salzburg, as well as Provost of the Frauensaal
church in Kärnten and of Isen in Bavaria; also Privy
Councilor to His Esteemed Grace of Salzburg and President
of the Spiritual Offices, My Gracious, High and Mighty
Lord, Most Venerable, Illustrious and Noble Imperial
Count, Gracious, High and Mighty Lord:

L: most renowned

L: Blessed Virgin Mary

L: + and most renowned
F: + and Prince of Salzburg
I: + His Highness, the
Archbishop and Prince of
Salzburg
L: + and benevolent patron
of the arts
L: + of the S.R.I.[1] and
Archbishop of Salzburg
F: Sir:
L: I dedicate and give into
Your Holy Hands
I: to Your Holy Hands
L: omit "I present . . . you."

If I submissively offer up to Your Esteemed Grace this
musical work consisting of my meager compositions,

I present nothing which does not already belong to you.
Inspired by the radiance of your graciousness, this work has
finally come to the light of day, and owes whatever
agreeable things it contains to yourself alone.
It was upon your noble recommendation that

L: in art and elegance
F: If I take the liberty to
dedicate to you this product
of my meager genius, I offer
you nothing which does not
belong to you. It is now
brought forth, inspired by
the radiance of Your Grace.
It owes all it can have of art
and beauty to you.
F: + , Archbishop and Prince
of Salzburg[2]
F: + he liberty to
F: mix
F: where I learned the
Italian sadness

His Serene Eminence of Küenburg of glorious memory
permitted me to explore Italy, where I strove to

moderate the melancholy Italian affects with the French

festivity and beauty in such a way that the one might not be

L: the Italian heaviness
F: omit "festivity and"

S.R.I. = Sancti Romani Imperi = Holy Roman Empire.
Maximillian Gandolph von Küenburg, Archbishop of Salzburg
from 1668 to 1687.

too dark and pompous, nor the other too free and boisterous. It is a telling indication of Your Grace's highly elevated virtue that, as an extrordinary example, the splendor of your most respected ancestry (in which kings are counted among your ancestors) is so laudably accompanied by the humility of a truly spiritual way of life, that your operation of the Court is accompanied by piety, and that your mind, which is well-versed in all matters of the intellect, is accompanied by a pure heart. It would be too little for your most laudable generosity to pour out your favors on me alone, if you had not also inundated my family with them for the past twenty years. When evil Jealousy sharpened its poisonous fangs on us, it learned to fear a Hercules in Your Grace,

F: too dismally heavy
L: seems to me

F: + not to say a miracle,
I: omit "(. . .)"

F=L=I: + Your Grace understands how to see himself raised in honor without neglecting the simple people, how to keep the secrets of counsel without compromising honor, and understands that in all his prosperity, the crown on his coat of arms is adorned with the cross.
L: + infamous

who ripped out the throat of the monster. As the waves of repugnance against us towered high, we held fast to your gracious protection as if to a secure anchor, awaited calm seas out of danger, and after the storm found the sunshine all the more pleasant. When the weak loyalty of changeable friends wavered and an estrangement threatened, we ceaselessly sensed, and humbly honored, in Your Grace a gracious patron, as we have to this very moment. May he deign to look with ever-gracious eyes on this poor token of the gratitude I owe for his generosity, printed here for all to see. I am not ashamed to be devoted to Your Grace; indeed I boast that I have nothing of my own which does not belong to you. One thing remains for me and mine: namely, to venerate with undying devotion the many favors shown to our unworthy selves, and to ceaselessly pray to the all-benevolent God to keep your most treasured Person in complete health and prosperity for countless years, as a most glorious light of your Church.

L: the clouds of Phœbus

F: omit "and humbly honored"

F: as constant as he is generous
F: this very day

I: omit "as . . . Church"

This I fervently desire and yearn for,
Your Grace's humble and obedient servant,
Georg Muffat.

F: These are the wishes I do not hesitate to utter, and I commend myself to the honor of Your Grace and to your protection. I remain with greatest respect,
I: With deepest bow, I remain, until I fall to ashes,

FOREWORD

After the publication of my two Bouquets or *Florilegia* of lovely ballet pieces,
the first in Augsburg in1695 and the second in Passau in 1698,
I now present to you, well-meaning Reader, this first collection of my instrumental concertos of choicest harmony, both serious and light-hearted; so named because it not only contains intact the brisk liveliness of the ballet arias which spring from the Lullian fountain, but also

> L: + for the reader of judgment
>
> L: omit "or *Florilegia*"
> L: instrumental pieces
> L: omit "in Augsburg"
> L: omit "in Passau"
> F: my dear Reader
>
> L: + dance-like
> L: modulations, commonly called Arias or Ballets

contains certain melancholy, exquisite affects of the Italian manner, assorted humorous artistic ideas, and various sorts of carefully arranged alternations of the large choir and the solo trio. These concertos, since they were composed only for the particular delight of the ear, can be most fittingly performed for (above all) the amusement of great Princes and Lords, and for the entertainment of prominent guests, grand meals, serenades, and gatherings of music-lovers and virtuosi; they are suitable for neither the Church, because of the ballets and other arias which they contain, nor for dancing, because of the alternation of slow and tragic passages with lively and nimble ones.

> L: heavy
> F: passages of Italian pathos
> F=L: + (Italian jokes)
>
> F: + connoisseurs and I: omit "music-lovers"
> F: omit "and virtuosi"

The first thoughts of this ingenious mixture came to me some time ago in Rome, where I was learning the Italian style on the keyboard under the world-famous Bernardo Pasquini, when I heard

> L: + noble
> L: once
> L: Italy's most famous player on the organ and the Apollonian harpsichord
> I=L: + , my honored master,

with great excitement and amazement

> F: omit "with great excitement"
> L: + of the ears
> L: + of the spirit

some concertos of

> F: *Symphonies*
> I: sonatas

the talented Archangelo Corelli

> I: + , the Italian Orpheus of the violin

performed most beautifully and with great precision by a large number of instrumentalists.
As I noticed the many contrasts in those pieces, I composed some of these present concertos, and I tried them out in the home of the above-mentioned Archangelo Corelli to whom I feel greatly obliged for generously conveying to me many useful observations concerning this style); and

> F: very well performed
>
> F: As I noticed the great variety in those pieces, which is richly present in this style,
> L: As I noticed that those pieces are rich in contrast,

with his approval, I was the first to bring some samples of this hitherto unknown harmony to Germany, just as previously, upon my return from France, I was the first to

introduce the Lullian Ballet style. I have increased the number of these pieces to twelve concertos, which were favorably performed on the most dignified occasions at various times and are explained by the mysterious titles placed before each concerto. These meager compositions of mine were granted hearings by His Most Gracious Imperial and Royal Majesty and by certain gracious Electors and other Princes, in Vienna, in Augsburg at the royal Coronation, and also in Munich, Salzburg, and Passau; the great favor (of which I am unworthy) freely conferred on them by these persons, as well as the approval of the most famous masters of exquisite discrimination and the acclaim of listeners (which is spreading also in distant lands), will easily comfort me when critics and jealous people come out against this work, people whose wicked efforts have always preceded a fortunate outcome for me. May you then, understanding Reader, sample this First Collection with a benevolent soul, and observe the following remarks, so that you might achieve my desired goal and achieve the full effect of these compositions in performance.

On the Number of Musicians and Instruments, and Their Characteristics

1. If you have few violinists, or if you would prefer to try these concertos with only
a few, then you will form a complete, indispensable trio from the following three parts:

Violino 1. Concertino, Violino 2. Concertino, and *Basso*

Continuo e Violoncino. It is better to play this bass part on a small French bass than on the *violone* commonly used here;

Marginal variants:

F: mixture

F: + , upon my return from Italy,
F: the style of M. de Lully's Ballets
I: French Ballet style

F: with their exquisite judgment
F: omit "of . . . discrimination"

F: taste
L: try
F=L: + scrupulously
F: achieve my intentions and attain the full strength
F: playing these concertos

I: players
F: hear
F: + instrumentalists
F: crucial and indispensable
I: *terzetto*
I: in each case omit "*Concertino*"
I: omit "and *Violoncino*"
I: + *Violoncino* or
F: *petite Basse à la Françoise*
I: *Basso Francese*
F: double or large bass, which one calls *violone*
I: + or Contrabass
L: so-called *violone*

to this is added a harpsichord or theorbo (which is played from the same part), for the greater embellishment of the harmony.

G: *Instrument*
F=I=L: + or a similar instrument
F: + as the bass instrument
I: omit "(. . .)"

Something else to observe is that along with *forte* and *piano*, passages marked T. (*tutti*) should be strong, but those marked S. (*solo*)

F: the exact observance of loud and soft at the words *forte* and *piano*, or simply at the letters f. and p., which indicate the same
F: + with the sign
F=I: + played
F: + or
F=I: + played
F: soft

should be quiet and gentle.

2. You can make music with four parts if you add *Viola 1.* to the principal parts described above, or with five parts if you also add *Viola 2.*

F: *Concert à quatre*
F: omit "with four parts"
G: *Geigen*

3. If still more musicians are available, you may add to those parts already named the remaining ones, that is *Violino 1.*, *Violino 2.*, and *Violone or Harpsichord* of the *Concerto Grosso* (or large choir), and assign whatever number of musicians per part seems reasonable, with either one, two, or three players per part. In this case a large *violone* would serve the majestic harmony of the bass quite well.

F: + *Concerto grosso*

I: omit "(or large choir)"
L: + as it is called in Italian

I: + or contrabass
F: a double bass, which the Italians call contrabass or *violone*, would serve well to express the bass of the large choir with the greatest majesty.
L: a bass violin, commonly called *violone*, or contrabass in Italian, or double bass in French, would serve quite well.

4. If, however, you have an even greater number of musicians at your disposal, you can increase the number of players per part for not only the first and second violins of

the large choir (*Concerto grosso*), but also, with discretion,

both the middle violas and the bass, and to adorn these with

F: + *dessus* or
F: + indicated
I: omit "(*Concerto Grosso*)"
L: + always indicated by the Italian words
F: one part or the other, *Taille* or *Viole du milieu*
F: + of the large choir

the accompaniment of harpsichords, theorbos, harps, and similar instruments.
However, the small choir or trio which is always indicated by the word *Concertino* should ideally be played with only one per part by your

three best players, with the accompaniment of an organist or theorbist, each part being played by the most accomplished musician, and never with more, except in very expansive halls where the larger choir is generally bigger, where they should be played with at most two per part.

F: several harpsichords
L: *Cithara*
L: *Triphonium*
F: the three parts of the small choir or principal trio (*Concertino*)
I: the *Concertino*
G: *Geigern*
F: only one harpsichord

F: + According to your discretion, you should fill out the first part of the large choir as well as possible, and also the first and second *dessus* (of the *concerto grosso*) as well as the middle parts. In the same way, the bass of the large choir (*violone* and harpsichord *Concerto grosso*) should be strengthened with as many small instruments as with large or "double" basses, and with others such as bassoons (*fagoto*) and *Bombardes*, and with instruments of accompaniment such as harpsichords, theorbos, harps, or regals.
I: It depends on your discretion whether to double the noble parts of the *Concerto grosso* and the middle voices, and to strengthen the bass as well as possible with *violones* and contrabasses, as well as with more cellos and bassoons.
L: I leave it to your discretion whether to have a few more players on the first and second violin parts than on the middle viola parts, or to enrich the bass with large violins or with small ones or with other instruments such as bassoons.

5. If some of your musicians can play the French oboe or shawm well, you can form the Concertino or trio with two of the best of these instead of the two violins, and with a good bassoonist instead of the small bass, and successfully use this group in certain concertos or selected Arias, if you select only concertos in keys convenient for those instruments (or if you transpose the concertos to those keys);

L: + *Tibia*
G: *Schalmei*
L: omit "the *Concertino*"
L: *Basso continuo*
F: If you have fine oboists among your musicians, you can use as the three voices of your trio or small choir (*Concertino*) two *dessus* and a bassoon

when the parts happen to go a bit too high or too low, the winds must be replaced by the violins, or must be transposed to a comfortable octave.

F: some small passages which exceed the range of the instruments must be altered

I have performed the first, second, third, fourth, and eighth concerti in this way in their original keys, but the ninth {sic}, in E major, I have often happily performed in E-flat major.

F: first, third, ninth, and tenth
I: first, third, fourth, eighth, ninth, and tenth
F=I: I have transposed the seventh from its key of E major to E-flat major, with the necessary changes.
F=I=L: + This is enough about what concerns the number and type of the musicians and instruments. We turn now to other, no less important, matters.
F: method

On the Manner Which Is to Be Observed in the Performance of These Concertos

F: playing

6. The very first note in the *Concerto grosso*, at the beginning or after a rest or breath, should be played strongly and bravely, without timidity, by each and every player, unless it is marked otherwise with the word *piano*. Otherwise, this note will weaken and darken the whole harmony if it is played sloppily or fearfully.

F: large choir

F: each musician and the whole ensemble
F: + strength and beauty of the

7. When *piano* or *p.* is marked, everyone together should become so soft and quiet that one one can hardly hear the ensemble, and when *forte* or *f.* is marked, everything from the first note on should be played so strongly that the listeners are astonished at such fullness.

F: + the word
F=L: the letter which means the same
F: + with such precision
L: + that one can hardly hear that the players are still touching the strings

8. As for the direction of the meter or measure, the Italian manner is mostly to be followed, in which passages marked with the words *Adagio, Grave, Largo,* etc. are taken much

more slowly than our musicians would play, sometimes to such an extent that one can hardly believe it. However, those marked *Allegro, Vivace, Presto, Più Presto* and *Prestissimo* are taken much livelier and faster. Then, through the rigorous observation of this opposition or contrast between slow and fast, loud and soft, the fullness of the large choir and the tenderness of the trio, the ear will be transported to a state of special amazement, just as the eye is so transported by the contrast of light and shadow. This cannot be said and urged enough, although it has often been repeated by others.

9. Each part, and thus the middle and lower parts as well, should be played not just by bad or weak violinists, but also by some good ones, who should not be insulted to be assigned to these parts which are as worthy as the others, contrary to the ingrained bad attitude of many self-important musicians who are affronted if they are not

assigned to the first violin part or a more important part.

10. The Italian manner is mostly to be followed in the opening *Sonatas,* the fugues, and the tender *Graves* which are mixed in: syncopations, notes which begin a tie, notes which form a dissonance with another part, and notes which resolve a dissonance (as those experienced in the art already understand) must always be played strongly, and preferably by lifting the bow from the string (*staccato* in Italian), since a horrible echo weakens them.

F: + with the exception of the Airs, which more nearly follow the *mouvement François*
F: ponderously

I: *Presto,* etc.
F: + than one is accustomed to here in these lands
L: omit "or contrast"
F: + beautiful
F: simple trio

F: Despite the laughable arrogance of those who scorn to play a part other than first violin, you should be sure to assign capable violinists to the middle parts as well as the others, so that these parts will be lively and secure, and the harmony will be completely perfect in all the parts.
I: omit "or a more important part"
F: *Symphonies (Sonatas)* which begin each concerto
F: + Airs in which
F: + of composition

F: with a bold, strong, and firm bowstroke, and *detaché* (*staccato* in Italian)
I: *staccato*
F: a weak and dull bowstroke
F: + In the Airs, it is best to follow the French manner in all its purity, the rules of which I have presented in my second *Florilegium.*
I: + In the Arias and Balletti, one must bear in mind the

11. Since most of the power and gratification of these compositions depends on the connections between one thing and that which follows, one must be diligent to avoid a noticeable pause or silence after a *Sonata, Aria,* or internal *Grave,* much less an irksome tuning of the violins, which interrupts this interdependent order; rather, it is to be earnestly requested that one hold out the final notes of internal sections only for their full written values, and otherwise follow the repeat pattern as usual, that is, the serious Arias are repeated only twice, the more lively ones occasionally three times, and the Graves not at all. Thus the listener should be kept in a constant state of attention, from the beginning to the end, until in an instant, unexpected by anyone, the concerto is over.

12. Finally, since nothing is as splendid or exalted, and thus is not valued, if it is heard too often, and since one may well surmise that this work will not fail to find the sort of eager bungler who will improperly put in *forte* and *piano,* *solo* and *tutti,* and other such markings here and there, who will dream, with a disorderly abundance of empty poses, to have reached the pinnacle of Art, my advice is not to play these concertos too often, and not to play two or more of them consecutively in a short period of time; rather, they should be performed only once, with grace and splendor, after another Partita in the usual style (of which there are many in my *Florilegia*),

properly observing the differences in the keys, and rehearsing beforehand in private, to bring a notable social function to an end with the greatest zeal.

If you have considered all this well, understanding Reader,

French manner of the late Mr. Lully in all its purity, the rules of which I have given in my second *Florilegium* or Second Selection of Ballets.
L: In the Arias or Ballets in the Lullian-Gallian manner, all the rules which I have written down in my *Florilegium Secundum* must be surely and elegantly observed in all their purity.
F: beauty

F: the unbreakable bond of the former with the latter
F: instruments
F: + on the contrary

F=L: + with all their repeats
F: or *intermèdes*, which are not Airs
F: all together and in the same instant, everyone ends and unexpectedly breaks off.

F: + without ability or understanding

F: + for the clever music director

F: omit "with . . . splendor"
L: after some pages of general dances (*Partien* in French), such as works from my *Florilegia*
F=I: omit "properly . . . keys"
F: (well-rehearsed and studied beforehand)
I: (very well-rehearsed)
F: omit "to bring . . . zeal"
F: my dear

may you look benevolently on this work, and await my
Florilegium Tertium or Third Bouquet of Ballet Pieces, and   F: omit "or . . . Pieces"
other works.
Farewell.   L: + and be blessed.

INDEX OF THE CONCERTOS
CONTAINED IN THIS WORK

First Concerto in D, called *Bona Nova* (Good News, in German), which was composed in Salzburg in 1698.

F:=L: + natural
L: + *dictus*
L: omit (. . .)
F: omit "was composed"

Second Concerto in A major, *Cor Vigilans* (or Watchful Heart), done in Rome in 1682.

L: + *intitulatus*
L: omit (. . .)

Third Concerto in B minor, *Convalescentià* (Convalescence), devised in Salzburg in 1683.

L: + *nuncupatus*
L: omit (. . .)

Fourth Concerto in G minor, *Dulce somnium* (Sweet Dream), composed in Rome in 1682.

L: + vocatus
L: omit (. . .)
L: completed

Fifth Concerto in D major, *Sæculum* (Hundred-Year Memory), completed in the same place and year.

L: + *appellatus*
L: omit (. . .)
I: in the same year in Rome
L: completed there in the same year

Sixth Concerto in A, called *Quis hîc?* (Who Is There?), Salzburg 1689.

L: + *nominatus*
L: omit (. . .)

Seventh Concerto in E major, or, if you prefer, in E-flat major, as indicated in the Foreword, called *Deliciæ Regum* (Royal Festivities), also composed in Salzburg in 1688.

L: + assembled in
L: + around
L: + with the title
L: + *fortitus*
L: omit (. . .)

Eighth Concerto in F, *Coronatio Augusta* (Majestic Coronation), likewise prepared in Salzburg in 1689.

L: + dictus
L: omit (. . .)

Ninth Concerto in C minor, *Victoria mæsta* (Sad Victory), in Salzburg in 1688.

L: + *intitulatus*
L: omit (. . .)
L: + worked out

Tenth Concerto in G, *Perseverantia* (Perseverance), arranged partly in Rome and partly in Salzburg.

L: + *nuncupatus*
L: omit (. . .)

Eleventh Concerto in E, called *Delirium Amoris* (The Madness of Love), composed in Rome.

L: + *vocatus*
L: omit (. . .)

Twelfth Concerto, once again in G major, called *Propitia Sydera* (Favorable Star), was brought to this order partly in Rome and partly in Salzburg.

L: + *apellatus*
L: omit (. . .)

INDEX OF THE AUTHOR'S WORKS IN PRINT

1. *Apparatus Musico-Organisticus*, most humbly dedicated
to our unconquerable, all-gracious Emperor LEOPOLDO
the First, for the most glorious coronation
of Her Majesty the Roman Empress and His Majesty the
Roman Emperor. This great royal work, decoratively
engraved in copper and published at great expense, was
most humbly placed in the hands of His Serene Highness
our Almighty Emperor by the author, was most graciously
heard by His Imperial Majesty, and was received with the
richest gift of grace. It contains twelve pieces .

> L: omit "all-gracious"
> L: + ever-
> L: of the spouse and the son
> F: omit "great royal"
> F=I: + 1690
> L: + in Augsburg

which the organists call *Toccatas*. Three other lively pieces
are included, namely a *Ciacona*, a *Passacaglia*, and a new
Blacksmith-Aria and its variations. The connoisseur of this

> F: organ pieces
> I: *Toccatas*
> F: Italians
> L: + are commonly
> I: omit "which . . . *Toccatas*"
> I: omit "Three . . . pieces"
> F: *Cyclopejade* or an allusion
> to the hammer of the
> Cyclops or the blacksmith.
> I: *Cyclopejade* or Aria,
> alluding to the hammer-
> blows of the blacksmith
> L: *Cyclopejade* of new
> harmony
> I: the keyboard art
> L: It offers therein abundant
> practice of the organist's art

art will find therein abundant practice. This work is
available from the author, from Georg Adam Höller, Book-
printer here, and also from Johann Baptist Mayr, Court and
Academic Printer in Salzburg.

2. *Suavioris Harmoniæ Instrumentalis Hyporchematicæ
FLORILEGIUM PRIMUM*, or First Bouquet of Lovely
Ballet Pieces, which contains fifty pieces for four or five
strings along with *Basso continuo* (if you wish), mostly
arranged in the French manner. It was printed in Augsburg
by Jakob Koppmayr and can be found at the shop of
Wilhelm Pannecker, bookseller there.

> F: + *à la Françoise*
> L: omit "or . . . Pieces"
> L: *modulationen* in the
> dance style, commonly
> called "*Balet*"
> G: *Geigen*
> F: omit "mostly . . . manner"

3. *Suavioris Harmoniæ Instrumentalis Hyporchematicæ
FLORILEGIUM SECUNDUM*, or Second Bouquet of
Lovely Ballet Pieces, containing nearly

> L: + for sale
> L: omit "or . . . Pieces"
> F=I=L: + in the same style,
> for four or five violins, with
> *Basso continuo* if you wish
> F: + new

the same number of pieces in the style of the previous work, composed in Passau for the stately reception of distinguished guests and for the ballet practice of the noble youth, and to which are added certain useful remarks in four languages concerning the manner in which to perform such pieces gracefully. It is printed by Georg Adam Höller and is available from him.

L: as in the *Florilegium Primum*

I: + in Passau
L: + in 1698
L: + for sale
F: More similar collections in the same style

More of the same works, God willing,

should follow in their own time with this title, always including some nice things of interest.

F: omit "follow"
L: + in order
F=I=L: *Suavioris Harmoniæ Instrumentalis Hyporchematicæ Floriligium* etc.
F: + *Œuvre de Concerts*, or

4. Then, in the present, this *Exquisitioris Harmoniæ Instrumentalis Gravi-Jucundæ SELECTUS PRIMUS*, or First Collection of Select Instrumental Music, both serious and light-hearted. If this work is benevolently accepted, the third Bouquet, which indulges in many other works still more unusual, and is arranged as much for the enjoyment of the ear as for theoretical usefulness, should soon follow, if Almighty God graciously lends me life and

L: omit "or . . . light-hearted"

I: + by you, good Reader

I: + , Giver of all good things,
L: + here, as in all places and all times, at the

strength. To whom be eternal praise and honor, our desired goal and END.

Part Three

Commentary

Chapter 5

Muffat's Intentions

eorg Muffat was one of the most cosmopolitan composers of the seventeenth century. Born of Scottish and French ancestry in Alsace, an area where French and German cultures overlapped, he studied music in Paris and law in Germany, traveled to Vienna, Prague, and Augsburg, worked in Alsace, Salzburg, and Passau, and spent a professional sabbatical in Rome. An educated man, Muffat was not only a performer, composer, and *Kapellmeister*, but was a rhetorician at the university in Molsheim, spoke at least German, French, and Italian (with a knowledge of Latin, of course), and was responsible for overseeing the education of noble children at the court of Passau.

Muffat, who had become intimately acquainted with three distinct national styles of music, believed that a mixing of several styles of music was generally beneficial to the result. Although his claim to have been the first to bring the French orchestral style to German-speaking countries may have been exaggerated—other German musicians, such as Fux, were learning about the French style around the same time—he was undoubtedly *among* the first, and in some of the places he visited was possibly the only musician to have studied in Paris. Likewise, his claim to have been the first to introduce the nascent Italian concerto style to Germany may be an exaggeration, although his *Auserlesene Instrumentalmusik* was, in fact, among the very first publications of concerti in Europe. Muffat's motivation for transmitting the French and Italian styles to German musicians no doubt derived in part from having something unique to offer; however, his writings hint at a deeper belief that a combination of elements from various musical styles could produce music more profound and delightful than anything which came from any single national style. In the dedication of his *Auserlesene Instrumentalmusik* to Maximilian Ernst von Scherffenberg, Muffat wrote:

> I strove to moderate the melancholy Italian affects with the French festivity and beauty in such a way that the one might not be too dark and pompous, nor the other too free and boisterous.

Similarly, he stated in the Foreword to that publication that the concertos contain both Italian-style movements and French-style dances intermingled with each other, and that "the Italian manner is mostly to be followed in the opening Sonatas, the fugues, and the tender Graves," while "in the Airs it is best to follow the French manner in all its purity." Although Muffat was concerned enough that performers of his *Florilegia* understand the Lullian style "in all its purity" to include a lengthy and detailed treatise on that style in the second publication, a passage from the dedication of *Floriligum Primum* to Count Johann Philip von Lamberg shows that his larger goal in that publication as well (and presumably also in *Florilegium Secundum*) was a unification of styles:

> . . . I dare not employ only a single style or method, but rather the most skillful mixture of styles I can manage through my experience in various countries. Not only one style, but a gathering-together of the best styles of various nations would be appropriate in order to amuse you with different forms of music and manners of playing.

Muffat fervently believed that a mixing of musical styles was the way to achieve an ideal music. This philosophy of "les goûts réünis" was championed by François Couperin and the French *Sonatistes* in the early eighteenth century, and did achieve great popularity, but Muffat obviously encountered considerable resistance to this approach in his own career. He wrote in the dedication to *Florilegium Primum*:

> Had these flowers been set out and planted in some other place, they could never have prospered; the roots would have been all but smothered, either because of harmful shade from envious branches, or through the spite of awful storms, had not Your Esteemed Grace shown them favor and freed them from the sand and the unfruitful clods, and set them out in his Passau garden bed.

This passage suggests that Muffat's interest in introducing the French style to Germany was not received with universal acceptance; indeed, Archbishop Johann Ernst von Thun, Max Gandolph's successor, was known to hate all things French. Another reference to the lack of acceptance of Muffat's music in certain quarters can be found in the dedication to *Auserlesene Instrumentalmusik*:

> When evil Jealousy sharpened its poisonous fangs on us, it learned to fear a Hercules in Your Grace, who ripped out the throat of the monster. As the waves of repugnance against us towered high, we held fast to your gracious protection.

Clearly, after having encountered hostility elsewhere, Muffat found in Passau a climate favorable to his interest in French and Italian music.

Although Muffat's remarks in the *Florilegia* attempt to convey an authentic French performance practice to German musicians, he did make some concessions to German practice, perhaps to increase the chances that the *Florilegia* would be performed by German ensembles. For example, the upper part (Violino) is notated in treble clef, rather than in French violin clef. While he recommends the use of violas for the three inner parts in accordance with the French practice, he does not rule out use of the violin for the violetta part, and kept the range of that part in the violin range as well; this must have been to account for situations in which the disposition of a particular orchestra would necessitate two violin parts and two viola parts. Muffat also notated the three inner parts in soprano, alto, and tenor clefs, following the German and Italian practice rather than the French (in which the inner parts are normally in soprano, mezzo-soprano, and alto clefs).

Muffat's musical philosophy also had a parallel in his social philosophy. Muffat had narrowly escaped being caught in a war zone when the armies of Louis XIV devastated the Alsace region during France's war with the Triple Alliance (see biographical sketch), and his life spanned a period in which wars were fought on a regular basis (usually involving France). His writings contain hints of a deep longing for peace, and a hope that music incorporating elements from several cultures might serve as a bridge between peoples:

> Since I had my start in France with the most experienced masters of this art of music, I realize that I could be accused of favoring that nation more than is appropriate, and in this time of war with France I could be considered unworthy of the kindly disposed ear of the Germans. . . . The weapons of war and the reasons for them are far from me; notes, strings, and lovely musical tones dictate my course, and as I mix the French manner with the German and Italian, I do not begin a war, but perhaps rather a prelude to the unity, the dear peace, desired by all the peoples.

In other words, Muffat is telling his readers that if the musical styles of several nations can be combined to produce something wonderful and harmonious, surely there is hope that people of different nations can coexist in peace and harmony. In addition, the conclusion of Muffat's First Remarks in *Florilegium Secundum* includes this statement:

> And so, well-meaning Reader, . . . pray to [GOD the Almighty] to grant quiet times, favorable for the Muses, to his Christendom and especially to our Germany.

Finally, Muffat used botanical imagery in the dedications of the *Florilegia* to refer to his compositions, comparing them to flowers blooming in a garden, nourished by soil, water, and sunshine, and collected in a bouquet or "Florilegium." He could scarcely have offered a more peaceful metaphor for his work.

Chapter 6

Instruments

French Style

In the titles of all three publications, Muffat uses the word *Geigen* when referring to the instruments played. Some seventeenth-century sources, such as Johann Gottfried Walther, seem to use the word to mean "bowed string instrument"; Walther used the word in his definition of the violetta, and went on to say that it could be an instrument played either *da braccio* or *da gamba*, and also used the word in his definition of the six-stringed violone. The Italian versions of the titles of both *Florilegia* use the term *stromenti d'arco*, and the Latin versions read *fidibus*, words meaning "stringed instruments" which could include instruments of the viol family. Praetorius, however, used the word *Geigen* to mean instruments of the violin family, and used the word *Violen* to refer to instruments of the gamba family.[1] Although Praetorius's work was considerably earlier than Muffat's era, it does represent an instance of *Geigen* specifically meaning "violin-family instruments" in a German publication. The word *Violons* in the French versions also helps support the interpretation of *Geigen* as "violin-family instruments"; Eppelsheim, referring to Mersenne and other sources, confirmed this meaning of "violons" in seventeenth-century France, and builds a case for the exclusive use of violin-family instruments in Lully's orchestra.[2] In the First Remarks of *Florilegium Secundum*, in which he discussed various aspects of the French dance style, Muffat again used the word *Geigen* to refer generally to the instruments of the ensemble; but in section IV (*Mos*) of the First Remarks in *Florilegium Secundum*, he wrote more specifically that "a somewhat more narrowly made viola would serve better for the Violetta part, which the French call *haute*

[1] Michael Praetorius, *Termini musici*, Syntagma musicum, vol. 3 (Wolfenbüttel: Elias Holwein, 1619; facs. ed., Kassel: Bärenreiter, 1988), pp. 122, 157.

[2] Jürgen Eppelsheim, *Das Orchester in den Werken Jean-Baptiste Lullys* (Tutzing: Verlag Hans Schneider, 1961), pp. 42–6. As the single exception to this practice, Eppelsheim writes that two *basses de viole* were used in the *petite chœur* of Lully's opera orchestra in Paris; they were used in the accompaniment of solo songs.

contre, than a violin." Whether a violin or viola is used, the instrument is of the violin family.

In the *Florilegia* suites, the top part (Violine) is to be played by the violin (the *kleine Geige*), while the three inner parts (Violetta, Viola, and Quinta Parte) are to be played by violas of different sizes. This corresponds to the French practice in which the three inner parts are played on instruments of different sizes but the same tuning of c g a' e" (see Eppelsheim), and are normally notated in soprano, mezzo-soprano, and alto clefs. Violetta is a word used commonly in seventeenth-century Germany, by composers such as Biber and Buxtehude, as a designation for an inner part in string music; precisely what instrument is meant by this word is unclear. Johann Gottfried Walther gave the word "violetta" as an alternative to "viola da braccio," and wrote that the instrument "is of larger structure and proportion than the violin, but nevertheless of the same nature, and is tuned a fifth lower, namely a. d. g. c."[3] Although Walther also gave a different definition of "violetta" which states that either violas [*Braccien*] or discant violas da gamba can play this part, Muffat's use of the word implies a violin-family instrument, especially since he does not rule out the possibility of playing the part on a violin. Muffat's intention is that the violetta part be played on a smaller instrument than the viola part; the French version of the passage above states that the violetta should be "smaller-made than the *Taille* (Viola)." He wrote that the part may be played on a violin, perhaps in the event that a smaller viola is not available, although he clearly prefers the part to be played on viola. Violas of different sizes, namely alto and tenor, would have been readily available in Germany for the Viola and Quinta Parte parts; in fact, in the "Instructions to the Bookbinder" from *Florilegium Secundum*, Muffat referred to the quinta parte as "Viola Tenore," a further indication that the large tenor viola is what he had in mind for that part.

The bass part, Muffat wrote,

> is given of necessity to the small bass violin [*kleine Bass-Geigen, petite Basse à la Françoise*], which the Italians call *violoncino* and the Germans call the French bass. (*Florilegium Secundum*, IV, 5)

Stampfl suggests that this instrument is the *basse de violon*, an instrument seldom used in Germany which had a tuning of $B\flat_1$ F c g.[4] Praetorius referred to the "normal bass violin" (*gemeine Baßgeigen*) as having the name "Bassviola" in Italian; both terms imply a member of the violin family. Praetorius did not refer to *petite Basse*, or to violoncino. Walther, however, gave the term "Bassa Viola" as an alternative for violoncello. Walther gave both *Basses de Violon* and *kleine Baß-Geigen* as alternatives for *Basset* (French) or *Bassetto* (Italian), and writes that these terms apply to "whatever part, or instrument, performs the *fundament* of a harmony in a high register (*in der Höhe*), in place of the proper bass."[5] Muffat's term *kleine Bass-Geigen*

---

[3] Johann Gottfried Walther, *Musikalisches Lexikon* (Leipzig: Wolffgang Deer, 1732; facsimile ed., Kassel: Bärenreiter, 1953), pp. 636–7.

[4] Stampfl, p. 36.

[5] Walther, p. 78.

is used by Walther in entries for "Basse de Viole," "Basse de Violon," "Basse petite," and "Violoncello"; the term "Basse petite" (*petite Basse à la Françoise* in Muffat) is defined by Walther as "a small *Baß-Geige* which sounds an octave higher than the large Violon[e]," a definition which further confuses the issue because Walther himself defines a violone as a six-stringed instrument. It would thus seem unlikely that Walther's *Basse petite* would be a four-stringed *basse de violon*; however, Walther's indiscriminate use of the word *Geigen* makes this difficult to ascertain. Thus, the terms *kleine Bass-Geigen* and *petite Basse à la Françoise* fail to provide clarity; Muffat's term *violoncino*, as well, is problematic because it appears in neither Praetorius nor Walther. Klaus Marx writes that "violoncino" is a word applied to the bass instrument of the violin family from about 1641, a diminutive of the term "violone," and that the term "violoncello" replaced it beginning around 1665.[6] He also points out that the tuning of this instrument was originally B♭, F c g, the tuning associated with the French *basse de violon*, but that the C G d a tuning, which was associated with the violoncello, was used beginning in the late sixteenth or early seventeenth centuries. The violoncello, which generally had a smaller body than the *violoncino* or *basse de violon*, seems to have appeared in the 1660s or 1670s, and seems not to have been the instrument which Muffat had in mind. The normal instrument in a German string ensemble was often a small *violone* at 8-foot pitch (see below under "Italian Style"), and Muffat was apparently expressing his preference for the violin-family *violoncino/ basse de violon* over the gamba-family *violone*.

The possible choices for Muffat's bass instrument, then, are: 1) a four-stringed *basse de violon*, possibly larger than a cello and tuned B♭₁ F c g; 2) a six-stringed member of the viol family, tuned G c f a d' g', an octave higher than the bass *violone*; 3) a cello, tuned C G d a, which Muffat refers to by the archaic name *violoncino*. Of these possibilities, the most likely choice is a four-stringed *basse de violon*, larger and lower-pitched than a violoncello. The *basse de violon* was the normal orchestral bass instrument in France until the 1710s; Lucy Robinson wrote: "The *basses de violon* made by Gaspar Borbon (c. 1700) are considerably larger than an 18th century cello and were probably played with the lower end resting on the ground."[7] This is undoubtedly the type of instrument with which Muffat would have become acquainted during his years of study in Paris; Eppelsheim concluded from the writings of Mersenne and Corrette, and from the ranges of Lully's bass parts, that the *basse de violon* was the instrument used in Lully's orchestra.[8] Furthermore, Muffat's use of the term *petite Basse à la Françoise* implies an instrument which was considered (at least by Germans) distinctively French, as the *basse de violon* was in the late seventeenth century. Marx suggests that the violoncello was in widespread use throughout Europe, except for France, by the time Muffat published his *Florilegia*, and the fact that Muffat did not use that term must be seen as significant. Finally, Muffat's concern that "the proportions of the harmony" would be distorted in the absence of this instrument also supports the use of a larger, deeper-sounding instrument than the violon-

[6] Klaus Marx, "Violoncello," in *The New Grove Dictionary of Music and Musicians*.
[7] Lucy Robinson, "Basse de violon," in *The New Grove Dictionary of Music and Musicians*.
[8] Eppelsheim, pp. 36–44.

cello, and a more powerful one than the 8-foot violone, for the bass line of a work with three inner parts; Eppelsheim wrote, "The tone of the *basse de violon* must have been stronger and more voluminous than that of the Violoncello; that was important, since the French orchestra in the time of Lully did not include a contrabass stringed instrument."[9] Stampfl also lists musicians associated with the Passau court and cathedral during Muffat's tenure there,[10] and among these is Simon Fischer, *Dommusiker* from 1687 to 1713 on violin, bass violin (*Baßgeige*), and bassoon; if the *Baßgeige* referred to is in fact the *basse de violon* rather than the violone, it is possible that Muffat was responsible for the hiring of a musician who played the instrument, or for the learning of the instrument by Fischer, in order to be able to include the *basse de violon* in his orchestra.

In a last word about the bass part, Muffat wrote:

> If there are a sufficient number of musicians, the large bass, which the Germans call
> *Violone* and the Italians call *Contra Basso*, will bring out a special majesty, although one
> of which the Lullists have not yet made use in the Ballets. (F2, IV, 5)

Praetorius grouped this instrument with the viol family, rather than the violin family, equating "violone" with the terms *Groß Baßgeig* and *groß Viol de gamba, oder Contrabasso da gamba*,[11] and referring to an instrument of five or six strings, tuned in fourths, whose lowest string is e or d, three octaves below middle c.[12] Walther also defined "violone" as a six-stringed instrument, tuned g, c, f, a, d, g, although he confuses the issue slightly by giving *Basse de Violon* as an alternate term for "violone." This could imply that the violone, despite its six strings, was considered the deepest instrument of the violin family. Rodney Slatford's article in the *New Grove Dictionary* also suggests that the violone or contrabass in seventeenth-century Germany was six-stringed and fretted, thus belonging to the viol family rather than the violin family, and played an octave below the cello or bass gamba.[13] In the seventeenth century, particularly in Germany, *violone* did not always imply an instrument at 16-foot pitch, but could be a generic term for a bowed bass instrument; Biber, for example, invariably calls the part which plays the bass line at 8-foot pitch "violone." It is clear from the context, however, that Muffat is referring to an instrument at 16-foot pitch. His interest in this instrument is due to his own personal preference, rather than reflecting French (Lullian) practice. French orchestras probably did not include contrabass stringed instruments until the first decade of the eighteenth century;[14] use of the more powerful *basse de violon* may have made use of contrabasses unnecessary, and the adoption of the contrabass roughly coincides with the replacement of the *basse de violon* with the violoncello.

---

[9] Eppelsheim, p. 42.

[10] Stampfl, p. 14.

[11] Praetorius, p. 122; and Michael Praetorius, *Die Organographia*, Syntagma musicum, vol. 2 (Wolfenbüttel: Elias Holwein, 1619; facsimile ed., Kassel: Bärenreiter, 1985), p. 44.

[12] Praetorius, *Organographia*, p. 25.

[13] Rodney Slatford, "Double Bass," in *The New Grove Dictionary of Music and Musicians*.

[14] Eppelsheim, p. 48–64.

Muffat's remarks about the French style say nothing about the use of wind instruments in the suites. However, Eppelsheim wrote that the normal configuration of the orchestra in the works of Lully and his contemporaries was violin-family strings with oboes and bassoon, and that passages in which the strings were to play without the winds (vocal solos with string accompaniment) were marked *violons seul* and occurred only in Lully's later works.[15] The normal sound of the Lullian orchestra that was Muffat's model, therefore, was that of strings with oboes and bassoons doubling the upper part and the bass. (Eppelsheim wrote that wind instruments, oboes, recorders, trumpets, etc., also played by themselves during trio-texture sections such as *ritournelles*, and were used for dramatic effect in conjunction with stage action.) Thus, it may not be inappropriate to double the outer parts in Muffat's *Florilegia* suites with winds. Nevertheless, Muffat's lack of instructions to that effect, and his statement that the suites are for four or five *Geigen*, make such a practice debatable.

Muffat included part-books for basso continuo in both *Florilegia* publications; however, the titles of both works indicate that the pieces may be played with basso continuo "if you wish" (nach Belieben, se piace, si l'on veut, si lubei animandis). That Muffat could consider the basso continuo part optional rather than mandatory is due to the nature and function of the inner parts in French five-part texture. Eppelsheim wrote that the French orchestra in the seventeenth century was composed of two groups of instruments: the two outer parts, and the three inner parts. It is well known that Lully himself composed only the outer two parts; these two parts provide the essence of the piece, establishing the melody and the foundation. The function of the second (and secondary) group of the three inner parts was to accompany the outer voices and fill out the harmony. Indeed, Eppelsheim states that the inner parts function like a written-out continuo realization. In Lully's five-part music, these inner parts were composed by other musicians, such as Lallouette and Collasse.[16] Although continuo instruments were not used in Lully's *grand chœur*, presumably since the inner parts already provided a realization of the harmony, harpsichord and theorbo were employed in the *petite chœur*, which mostly accompanied vocal solos.

Muffat wrote that the suites of both *Florilegia* may be played "with four or five strings." Although he does not elaborate on the meaning of this phrase, an explanation may be found in his instructions on the number of players in the Foreword to *Auserlesene Instrumentalmusik*, in which he wrote that the five-part music of that collection may be played in four parts by leaving out the Quinta Parte or second viola part. This seems a reasonable interpretation for his instructions in the *Florilegia* as well. Eppelsheim wrote that Lully's contemporaries used a four-part texture, without a third inner voice, in contexts where a smaller ensemble would be expected (such as Pastorales, Divertissements, stage music, church music, etc.),[17] and he described how the normal five-part texture in Lully operas was reduced to four parts in the early eighteenth century, when the four-part texture was becoming standard, by simply eliminating

---

[15] Eppelsheim, p. 197.
[16] Eppelsheim, p. 179–83.
[17] Eppelsheim, p. 189.

the *quinte* or third inner part, without changing any of the other parts.[18] This practice most likely stemmed from an earlier convention with which Muffat became acquainted during his studies in Paris in the 1660s.

Muffat did not give specific instructions about the number of players who should perform the *Florilegia* suites. What he wrote is:

> The parts should be judiciously distributed and apportioned according to the number of musicians, so that one can distinguish and perceive everything well and beautifully. And all the best players should not be assigned to the violin (or upper) part, so that the middle voices seem robbed of the necessary players; this manner of harmony, whose grace is concealed in the lower parts, would be deprived. It is most regrettable that this often happens because of the ambition of certain tactless people to play the first part. (F2, IV, 4)

French orchestras in the seventeenth century varied widely in size and distribution; Mersenne gave the distribution of players in the 24 Violons du Roi as 6, 4, 4, 4, 6, an arrangement in which the two groups of players (outer voices and inner voices) are of equal size. However, Eppelsheim described Lullian orchestras for various productions as having a far smaller proportion of players on the inner parts, with as many as twelve players on each outer part and as few as two on each inner part. Muffat, however, clearly considered the inner parts to be crucial to the effect of the pieces, and, although he did not elaborate about the number of players on each part, his aim was that all parts be clearly heard. The "manner of harmony" he referred to may be the function of the inner voices as a written-out continuo realization, as discussed above; the skill with which the inner parts are constructed can add to or subtract from the grace and rhythmic charm of the piece, in addition to fulfilling a harmonic function, and Muffat seemed proud enough of his inner parts to want them to be heard.

Italian Style

As in the *Florilegia*, Muffat intended violin-family instruments to be used in the concertos of *Auserlesene Instrumentalmusik*, in accordance with the Italian practice he had learned from Corelli in Rome. Unlike the French practice in which the three inner parts are played on instruments of the same pitch but different sizes, the practice more common in Italy and Germany is followed in this publication, in which the large string group is divided into two upper parts (violins, in treble clef), two middle parts (violas, in alto and tenor clefs), and basso continuo. In addition, the forces are divided into a large group or "choir" (ripieno or "concerto grosso"), consisting of two violin parts, two viola parts, and "Violone e Cembalo," and a small solo group consisting of two treble parts and a bass part, with basso continuo.

Muffat's preferred instrument for the solo bass part is the violin-family violoncino/*basse de violon* discussed above, rather than "the violone commonly used here." Muffat's Foreword to

---

[18] Eppelsheim, p. 181–3. Eppelsheim futher explained that it was possible to dispense with this part without damaging the integrity of the piece because of the secondary importance of the inner parts compared with the outer parts.

Armonico Tributo, which contains earlier versions of the concertos of *Auserlesene Instrumentalmusik*, differs in its instructions on instrumentation from the later publication only in its assertion that the concertino bass part may be played on either violoncino or viola da gamba. The desirability of a violin-family instrument over a violone for this part is easily understood; since the solo bass instrument is often an equal partner with the two solo treble parts (see, for example, the third movement of Concerto XI), a powerful and agile instrument is required, one which will balance well with two violins. While Muffat's model for the concerti, Corelli's orchestra of the early 1680s, may have included violoncellos, Muffat does not use this term. Corelli himself first used the designation "violoncello" in his own concerti (published 1714); in his previous publications, Opp. 1–5, Corelli used the ambiguous word "violone" to refer to the bass instrument. Muffat's failure to mention the violoncello, and Corelli's own late use of that word, may be an indication that Corelli's orchestra of 1681–2 did not include the violoncello.

The instrument Muffat recommends *against* as the solo bass instrument, "the violone commonly used here," was certainly at 8-foot pitch. Although elsewhere Muffat uses the word violone to mean a contrabass instrument at 16-foot pitch, the solo bass parts in the concerti are clearly intended to be performed at the written pitch; the relationship between that part and the two upper solo parts would make no sense if the bass were played an octave lower. Both 8-foot and 16-foot violones were commonly used in German string ensembles in the seventeenth century. Kerala Snyder wrote:

> Two sizes of violone were in use in Germany during the seventeenth century. Praetorius pictures a "Violone, Groß Viol-de Gamba Bass" in plate VI and a "gar grosse Violn [sic] de Gamba Sub Bass" or "Groß Contra-Bas-Geig" in plate V of his *Theatrum Instrumentorum*. Jacob Stainer's 1669 price list also indicates two sizes of violone . . . Fuhrmann also mentions two instruments: "Violone, *Bass-Geige*. Violone Grosso, an *Octav-Bass-Geige* on which is found the 16-foot Contra-C."[19]

The smaller 8-foot violone was the typical bass instrument in the ensemble works of German composers such as Buxtehude, Biber, and Rosenmüller.

Finally, Muffat recommended using a large violone at 16-foot pitch on the ripieno bass-line when the ripieno violin parts are played.

Muffat's Foreword to *Auserlesene Instrumentalmusik*, unlike those of the *Florilegia*, specifically mentions the use of wind instruments when the ensemble is large. He did not refer to the collaparte doubling of the string parts by winds, as was the practice in the Lullian orchestra, but instead wrote:

> If some of your musicians can play the French oboe or shawm [Schalmei] well, you can form the *Concertino* or trio with two of the best of these instead of the two violins, and with a good bassoonist instead of the small bass, and successfully use this group in certain concertos or selected Arias, if you select only concertos in keys convenient for those instruments (or if you transpose the concertos to those keys).

---

[19] Kerala J. Snyder, *Dieterich Buxtehude: Organist in Lübeck* (New York: Schirmer, 1987), p. 371.

By 1698, when *Auserlesene Instrumentalmusik* was published, the oboe (which most likely appeared in the 1670s) had nearly supplanted the shawm in most European countries,[20] although the young Muffat no doubt heard orchestras with shawms in the 1660s. The term "French oboe" used by Muffat is one which writers of the late seventeenth and early eighteenth centuries, such as John Talbot, normally used to refer to the newer "hautbois." The French version of the Foreword also states that the ripieno bass may be doubled by bassoons and bombardes when a large ensemble is used; the bombarde is a bass member of the shawm family. It may be that Muffat means that whichever family of instruments is available, either oboes and bassoons or shawms and bombardes, is acceptable.

Muffat's instructions regarding basso continuo make it clear that a continuo group which includes chording instruments is not optional, as it is in the *Florilegia*, but is essential. In fact, it is clear that when the concerti are performed by a large number of players, divided into a small group (concertino) and a large group (ripieno), each group is to be accompanied by its own continuo instruments. For the concertino group, Muffat first wrote that a harpsichord or theorbo is to be added "for the greater embellishment of the harmony," but later wrote that the concertino group is to be accompanied by "an organist or theorbist"; apparently any of those three instruments, or perhaps a combination of them, are appropriate to accompany the concertino group. This continuo section suffices for ensembles of up to three players per ripieno part. When ensembles larger than this are used, Muffat wrote, continuo instruments can be added to the ripieno bass as well; several harpsichords, theorbos, harps, and regals can be used according to the director's discretion, as well as bass instruments such as additional *basses de violon*, contrabasses, and bombardes or bassoons.

Muffat gave a number of alternatives concerning the size of the ensemble that is to play the concerti, and gave instructions that are essentially identical to those in the Foreword of his earlier (1682) publication *Armonico Tributo*. The smallest configuration, he wrote, is a trio-sonata group consisting of the two concertino violins, the concertino violoncino/*basse de violon*, and one (or more) chording instruments as described above. The next larger configuration is four- or five-part chamber music, which is achieved by adding one or both ripieno viola parts to the concertino group. A true "concerto" configuration is achieved when one adds the ripieno violin parts "and assigns whatever number of musicians per part seems reasonable, with either one, two, or three players per part." This arrangement of parts forms complete solo and tutti groups and adds the contrast of few players versus many players, allowing for the full effect of "the unique alternations, interruptions, and skirmishes between the full choir and the small solo trio." Finally, one can expand each section of the orchestra (including, "with discretion, both the middle violas and the bass") to whatever size one wishes, adding continuo instruments as noted above. No matter how large the ripieno group becomes, however, the concertino parts "should ideally be played with only one per part by your three best players, with the accompaniment of an organist or theorbist." The only exception occurs when a performance is held "in very expansive venues where the larger choir is generally bigger," when

---

[20] David Scott, "Shawm," in *The New Grove Dictionary of Music and Musicians*.

up to two players per part may play concertino. In an additional remark concerning the distribution of the players, Muffat makes a comment similar to the one quoted above from *Florilegium Secundum*:

> Each part, and thus the middle and lower parts as well, should be played not just by bad or weak violinists, but also by some good ones, who should not be insulted to be assigned to these parts which are as worthy as the others.

Chapter 7

Pitch and Temperament

Pitch Levels

n the First Remarks of *Florilegium Secundum* (IV, 3), Muffat makes the following remarks about pitch:

> The pitch to which the Lullists tune their instruments is generally a whole-step lower, and in theatrical productions even one-and-a-half steps lower, than our German pitch. The so-called *Cornett-Ton* seems to them to be quite too forced and piercing. If it were up to me, and there were no reason not to do so, I would select the so-called *Chor-Thon* [I: the so-called "old *Chor-Thon*" which is a whole-step lower] because of its liveliness combined with sweetness, with somewhat thicker strings [than Germans use].

In his comprehensive study of pitch in the seventeenth and eighteenth centuries, *Pitch Standards in the Baroque and Classical Periods*, Bruce Haynes wrote the following:

> *Pitch* combines two separate coordinates: not only a frequency value (such as 440 Hz, for instance), but also a note name, such as "A." A-440 Hz is a pitch, as is G-440 Hz. . . . A pitch standard is a convention of uniform pitch that was understood, prescribed, and used by musicians in general at a given time or place.[1]

Muffat, then, is describing four different pitch standards in the above remark: *Cornett-Ton* (commonly used in Germany), the French chamber pitch, the French opera pitch, and *Chor-Thon* (the pitch Muffat recommends). By studying Haynes' careful review of theoretical writings and period instruments, one can define the pitch standards referred to by Muffat in the following way (frequencies refer to the note A):

1. *Cornett-Thon*, c. 460–470 Hz. Also called *Cammer-Thon* by Praetorius, this was the normal pitch for secular music in seventeenth-century Germany, the pitch to which instruments

---

[1] Bruce Haynes, "Pitch Standards in the Baroque and Classical Periods" (Ph.D. diss., Université de Montréal, 1995), p. 1.

and church organs were normally tuned.[2] By the eighteenth century, also called *Chorton* in Northern Germany.

2. *Chor-Thon*, c. 416 Hz. This pitch, which lies between *Cornett-Thon* and the French chamber pitch, is the one recommended by Muffat because it combines the "liveliness" of the higher pitch with the "sweetness" of the lower. By the eighteenth century, with the advent of the new French wind instruments (the oboe, bassoon, and traverso) which were made at this pitch, A=416 Hz. became known as *Cammerton* in northern Germany (see Quantz and Walther), since it had become the pitch to which instruments were normally tuned for chamber music, and the higher *Cornett-Thon* was also called *Chorton*, because that was still the pitch to which church organs were tuned. However, in southern Germany and Austria, where Muffat lived, this pitch of approximately A=416 Hz. continued to be called *Chor-Thon* well into the eighteenth century.[3]

3. *Ton de chambre*, c. 404 Hz. The normal French pitch for chamber music, "a whole-step lower than our German pitch," was used in France from about 1680 to 1800, and had analogs elsewhere in Europe as well.[4]

4. *Ton d'Opéra*, c. 393 Hz. For about a century, from roughly 1660 to 1750, this was the pitch for opera in Paris, "one-and-a-half steps lower than our German pitch."[5]

Muffat's writings in *Auserlesene Instrumentalmusik* make no mention of Italian pitch standards and make no recommendations concerning the pitch at which the concerti are best performed. It could be assumed, then, that the normal German pitch for instrumental music (*Cornett-Thon*, c. 460–470 Hz., based on Muffat's statement quoted above) would be appropriate—otherwise Muffat would have stated another preference. However, since Muffat specifically indicated that oboes and a bassoon could be used in the performance of the concerti (see Chapter 6, "Instruments"), an ideal choice of pitch for performance of the concerti might be *Chor-Thon*, c. 416 Hz., the pitch at which the French wind instruments played (and the normal instrumental pitch in Germany in the eighteenth century). As we have seen, Muffat had already expressed a preference for this pitch in *Florilegium Secundum*.

Temperament

Muffat did not indicate that a particular temperament would be more appropriate for either French-style or Italian-style music. It is therefore reasonable to assume that Muffat considered the temperaments commonly employed in Germany and Austria at the end of the seventeenth century to be acceptable for both styles. "Just" temperaments, or temperaments based on pure major thirds and octaves and impure fourths and fifths, were used in the seventeenth century throughout Europe. By the end of the century, examples of temperaments using a "circulating" system of distributing the comma were published by writers such as Andreas Werckmeister

---

[2] Ibid., pp. 180–6.
[3] Ibid., pp. 353–6.
[4] Ibid., pp. 108–12.
[5] Ibid., pp. 112–18.

(1691, 1697, 1707) and Johann George Neidhardt (1706, 1724, 1732), in whose systems the thirds most often used were purer than the least-used thirds;[6] these systems reflected ongoing experimentation in the seventeenth century aimed at retaining just intonation while allowing instruments to play in many keys.

Intonation

Regarding intonation, Muffat had little to say beyond an admonition to play in tune and to study with a good teacher (*Florilegium Secundum*, Remarks, 1). Although his additional comment

> I have noticed that the mistakes most often made by those who are still inexperienced, and who finger the strings improperly, are these: that when two pitches lie a half-step apart (such as *mi* and *fa*, a and B♭, B and C, or also F♯ and G, C♯ and D, G♯ and A, etc.), that the lower pitch (*mi* or ♯) is not played high enough, and the upper pitch (*fa*) is not played low enough.

is surprising in terms of playing in a just temperament, Muffat seems to be referring to the intonation mistakes made by amateur players, rather than making a statement about the proper inflection of half-steps.

J. Murray Barbour, *Tuning and Temperament: A Historical Survey* (East Lansing: Michigan State College Press, 1953), pp. 178–84.

Chapter 8

Techniques

Bowing Rules

*M*uffat's description of the French bowing conventions is among the most complete and detailed pictures of that practice which survives. The widespread use of a systematic approach to bowing seems to have been unique to France in the seventeenth century; Muffat wrote

> The Germans and the Italians do not agree with the Lullists, nor even to any great extent among themselves, in the matter of the rules for up- and down-bows. But it is well-known that the Lullists, whom the English, Dutch, and many others are already imitating, all bow the most important notes of the musical meter . . . in the same way, even if a thousand of them were to play together. (F2, Remarks, 2)

Although Bartolomeo Bismantova's *Compendio Musicale* (1677) contains systematic rules of bowing very much like those described by Muffat,[1] there is little evidence that these rules were generally adopted in Italy.

The reason for the existence of bowing conventions in French music is to achieve a uniform sound. The passage quoted above continues:

> Thus when noble men returned to our lands from these places [in which the Lullian practice is followed], and did not find this unanimity among our German violinists, who were otherwise excellent, they noticed the difference in the concord of sound and were amazed, and complained not infrequently about the improper movement of the dances.

Since that uniformity of sound was such a distinctive part of the sound of a French ensemble, Muffat needed to describe the bowing rules which led to that uniformity in order to bestow on his German readers as complete an understanding of French performance practice as possible.

---

[1] Stewart Carter, "Instructions for the Violin from an Overlooked Source: Bartolomeo Bismantova's *Compendio Musicale* (1677)," Ms., p. 2. From the author.

But the real motivation for Muffat's detailed and painstaking description of French bowings was not merely a desire for authenticity, but rather was the effect of those bowings on the way the music would be by the listeners. The passage quoted above, in addition to discussing the "concord of sound" typical of a French ensemble, mentions the "movement of the dances," as indicated (or mis-indicated) by the performance of the music. Muffat wrote that the Lullian manner of playing has two characteristics; first, that (like most French music of the Baroque) it is pleasing to the ear, and second,

> that it indicates the meter of the dance so exactly that one can immediately recognize the type of piece, and can feel the impulse to dance in one's heart and feet at the same time, contrary to all assumptions.

In other words, the listener can tell within a few notes, from the tempo, rhythm, articulation, and flow of the measure, whether the piece being played is an allemande, a gavotte, or a sarabande.

While each type of dance has certain characteristics of tempo and rhythm which help the listener identify it, a string player can signal the flow of strong and weak impulses in a measure or a phrase by the way he or she uses the bow. Muffat referred to this flow of impulses expressed by the bow:

> [The Lullists] all bow the most important notes of the musical meter, especially those which begin the measure and which end a cadence, and thus strongly show the motion of the dance, in the same way.

Indeed, all the rules of bowing described by Muffat are designed to impart strong and weak inflections to the music, and thus to "show" audibly the movements of whatever dance was being performed. Since down-bow is strong and up-bow is weak when playing with a baroque bow, conventions about up- and down-bows result in conventions of strong and weak inflections, based on the strong and weak parts of the measure and, as Muffat says, on the movements of the dance.

Italian-style music is not based on the movements of dance in the same way as French music. In *Auserlesene Instrumentalmusik*, Muffat gave the following instructions about when to make strong inflections:

> Syncopations, notes which begin a tie, notes which form a dissonance with another part, and notes which resolve a dissonance (as those experienced in the art already understand) must always be played strongly, and preferably by lifting the bow from the string (*staccato* in Italian), since a horrible echo weakens them.

The only surprise in this passage is the instruction to play the *resolutions* of dissonances strongly. This may be explained by considering the statement to be a caution against playing resolutions so weakly that the effect of dissonance/resolution is lost, as can sometimes happen with inexperienced players. The instruction to lift the bow from the string probably has more to do with allowing the note to ring (as opposed to dampening it with the bow on the string) than with the actual length of the strong note.

Articulation

In addition to strong and weak inflections, the flow and shape of a musical line is formed by the articulations employed. In *Florilegium Secundum*, Muffat referred to several kinds of articulation on stringed instruments, including repeated down-bows, repeated up-bows, slurs, staccato, up-bow spiccato, and staccato. Muffat also wrote the following about bow-strokes in general:

> . . . Good violinists [F: of all nations] hold that the longer, steadier, more even, and sweeter the bow-strokes, the better.

This refers to the basic sound produced on a stringed instrument, in which the bow moves smoothly, firmly, and evenly across the string. A beginning student or an untalented amateur might play with bow-strokes that are uneven or unsteady in terms of bow speed and contact with the string, producing an unpleasant and uneven sound as a result. Judging from several remarks scattered through his writings, Muffat had had some experience with such players, and in addition to detailed information about performance practice for the professional, he felt obliged to include a few references to basic technique as well.

Repeated Down-Bow

Muffat's Rule 3 on bowing states:

> Of the three notes which make up a whole measure in triple time, the first would be played down-bow, the second up-bow, and the third down-bow, when played slowly, according to Rule 1; this means one would play two down-bows in a row at the beginning of the following measure.

Since he had already established a principle of playing separate notes with alternating bow-strokes when time permits, and since Rule 1 states that the downbeat of a measure, being the most important part of the measure, should be played down-bow, the double down-bow of Rule 3 follows naturally. The same logic applies to Rule 5:

> If several notes follow one another, each of which comprises a whole measure, each one must be played down-bow.

An additional situation in which double down-bows may be used is given in Rule 7:

> As for unequal notes, the first of the smaller notes which follow the larger ones is considered odd-numbered, and one plays them . . . if the situation demands, with repeated down-bows.

Although the purpose for repeated down-bows is the same in all these examples, namely to create strong inflections, not all down-bows need be considered equally strong. Although Muffat did not extend his discussion of strong and weak beats in the section on ornamentation to the level of good and bad measures, this principle follows logically and is a basic technique of phrasing and articulation in Baroque music. Muffat did make the following statement:

> The greatest skill of the Lullists lies in the fact that even with so many repeated down-bows, nothing unpleasant is heard, but rather that they wondrously combine a long line with practiced dexterity, a variety of dance movements with the exact uniformity of the harmony, and lively playing with an extraordinarily delicate beauty.

This passage tells us that repeated down-bows were commonly used by French string players, but that the sound was not a clumsy and unmusical string of repeated strong impulses. A long line is achieved by shaping phrases with a variety of strongs and weaks and a variety of articulations, with arrival at a high point, and a building to and/or falling away from that high point. The French players observed by Muffat clearly performed in this manner, even using bowings which might to German musicians have seemed clumsy. Even when the playing was forceful or "lively," it is described as "delicate," meaning that the players controlled their bows so well that no harsh sounds resulted, thanks to their "practiced dexterity."

There are at least two ways of playing double down-bows on a stringed instrument. The first is to retake the bow at the end of the stroke and return it to the frog for the beginning of the next stroke; this would tend to make the second down-bow stroke a strong one, by playing it in the strongest part of the bow (the frog). The second is to begin the second down-bow at the same point on the bow at which the previous down-bow stopped; this technique would tend to make the second down-bow weaker than the first, since it would be played in a weaker part of the bow (assuming that the same speed and weight were applied to the bow on both strokes). Muffat did not specify which technique applies in specific situations, nor did he even distinguish between the two. This could be one situation in which his explanation was handicapped by the fact that he was not a string player himself; in the Foreword to *Florilegium Secundum*, he wrote:

> I would like to acknowledge, by the way, that someone who is a professional violinist, and well acquainted with the described manner (and there are already many of them in these lands), could have done this much better than I.

Each of these two ways of playing double down-bows produces a distinctive articulation. If the bow is retaken, it must be lifted from the string at the end of the first stroke before the second is played, which produces a silence (or a ringing) between the strokes. If the two strokes are the last beat and the first beat of two consecutive measures, as in the example of Rule 3, the first may be shortened in order that the second (the downbeat) may be played on time. If the second down-bow is played without a retake, however, the result is more of a pulsation than a clear articulation.

None of the examples given by Muffat which call for repeated down-bows (see musical examples D, L, O, T, V, and HH in *Florilegium Secundum*) illustrate situations in which the bow could not be retaken for the second down-bow stroke. However, the examples from Bismantova's *Compendio* (1677) call for repeated down-bows that could be performed only without a retake, due to the speed of the notes,[2] which indicates that such a stroke was part of the violinist's vocabulary of bowing techniques in the seventeenth century, at least in Italy.

---

[2] Carter, p. 5.

Repeated Up-Bow

Another type of bow-stroke described by Muffat is a double up-bow. Rule 3, concerning "the three notes which make up a whole measure in triple time," contains the following statement:

> If one plays faster, the second and third notes are often both played up-bow, the bow springing equally on each note [F: in which the stroke, called *craquer*, is divided exactly into two parts and should be executed with great lightness].

This description makes it clear that the second up-bow begins at the same point on the bow at which the previous up-bow stopped, and produces two notes which are separated from each other and lightly inflected. This stroke is recommended by Muffat in situations where repeated down-bows might be too heavy or might take too long. The notes played with this stroke are generally weak notes in the general hierarchy of the measure. Examples E, S, BB, HH, and NN show the use of this stroke.

An extension of the idea of the double up-bow stroke is found in the section on ornamentation (V, *Venustas*) from *Florilegium Secundum*:

> The *coruscation* ( ) is distinguished from the figured confluence only in that the notes are played distinctly, and, so to speak, with a hopping bow-stroke.

Slurs

Slurs are first mentioned by Muffat in Rule 10, in which he wrote:

> Finally, when two eighth or sixteenth notes are paired as a grace, they can either be played separately, or (which is more lovely) played together with one bow, as it seems appropriate.

This grouping of notes under a slur has the effect of articulating only the first note of the slur, which is desirable when the other notes under the slur are ornamental and should not be too important. However, Muffat cautioned about using slurring which obscures the articulation of notes which are important to the rhythmic integrity of the dance:

When one slurs the short note after a dot to the note which follows, breaking Rule 10 as shown in Example LL, this contradicts the liveliness of the music.

In this case, the dotted eighth notes which fall on the beats of the first measure, and the quarter note which falls on the third beat of the second measure, are not articulated (since they lie in the middle of a slur). If the beats of the measure are not articulated, the music no longer clearly shows the movement of the dance, departing from Muffat's goal.

Slurs are also mentioned in the section on ornamentation (V, *Venustas*) of *Florilegium Secundum*. Here, the slur is called a simple confluence:

> The *confluence* fluidly binds together two or more notes in one bow. It is *simple* or *figured*; the simple, which is notated ⌢ or ⌣ in the composition, includes no other notes.

The description of the confluence as "fluid" confirms that the notes within a slur are not articulated. Since the slur or "simple confluence" is given as an ornament, one has the liberty to add slurs to any passage if one takes care not to distort the rhythmic integrity as in Example LL. The example given by Muffat to illustrate the simple confluence preserves the articulation of each beat of the measure:

Staccato

Finally, Muffat referred to staccato articulation in the section on ornamentation (V, *Venustas*) of *Florilegium Secundum*:

> The staccato (.) is when each note is played as if it were followed by a rest.

Holding the bow and the violin

The type of articulations Muffat wished his readers to achieve were no doubt those he heard played by the string players of Lully's orchestra. The sound of those articulations may have been affected by the way in which the violin and bow were held by the players. Muffat wrote this about the way in which the bow is held:

> Most Germans agree with the Lullists on the holding of the bow for the violins and violas; that is, pressing the thumb against the hair and laying the other fingers on the back of the bow. It is also generally held in this way for the bass by the Lullists; they differ from the Italian practice, which concerns the small violins, in which the hair is untouched, and from that of the bass gambists and others, in which the fingers lie between the wood and the hair. (Fl2, Remarks)

Holding the bow in the Lullist manner, with the thumb under the frog rather than between the stick and the frog, can produce a much stronger contact with the string and much more powerful down-bow strokes than can be achieved with the "Italian" technique used by modern players. In fact, subtleties of bow strokes and repeated downbows using the "thumb under frog" grip are difficult for someone accustomed to the other type of grip to play without producing unpleasant sounds. However, Muffat specifically stated that "nothing unpleasant is heard" from the Lullists, whose "practiced dexterity" was achieved by years of practice, and to whom the "thumb-under" grip was natural. Nevertheless, it is likely that the Lullian string section, all bowing together and using this bow grip, made a very impressive sound on the strong notes; by all contemporary accounts, this was the case.

The manner in which the violin was held in France may also have affected the sound of the articulations. Until around the turn of the eighteenth century, when the Italian manner of playing the violin gained popularity in France, the instrument was mostly held on the chest, rather than on the neck or shoulder.[3] The effect on violin articulation when this type of position is used is generally a "softening" of articulation; the sound produced is more viol-like and less sharp. Since the bow-arm makes less of an angle with the string in this position, less of the weight of the arm is naturally transferred onto the string since the arm does not "hang" from the bow as much, the player relies more on the fingers of the bow hand to press the bow into the string. One result of this is that the difference between the strong down-bow and the weak up-bow becomes even more exaggerated. It was for this reason that the breast or "French" position was especially suited to the playing of dance music, where strong and weak inflections are so important.

Ornamentation

Muffat described ornamentation in the Lullian style in great detail in *Florilegium Secundum*, listing the "most important and essential" ornaments with examples and discussing their use.

---

[3] Boyden, p. 152.

His exposition and discussion on this topic is very clear and straightforward, and needs little commentary.[4] However, it is interesting to note that ornamentation was evidently a stumbling block for some musicians of Muffat's time who sought to learn the French manner of playing. Muffat's writings make it clear that while ornamentation is an important part of performance practice in the French style, it was often misunderstood and misapplied:

> Those who unreasonably hold forth that the Lullian violin ornaments only obscure the melody or are composed only of trills, have not properly considered the matter, or have never adhered to the true Lullists, but only to false ones. On the contrary, those who are immersed in the nature and variety, the beauty, the sublimity, and true origins of the proper use of the ornaments, which spring from the purest fountain of vocal technique, have to this day noticed nothing which hinders the distinction of the melody or the precision of the harmony.
>
> ... There are many different things which work against this most noble element of music, which certain idle scoffers consider useless: namely Neglect, Impropriety, Excess, and Incompetence. Through Neglect, the melody as well as the harmony becomes empty and unadorned; through Impropriety, it becomes hard and barbaric; through Excess, it becomes confused and ridiculous; and finally through Incompetence, it becomes awkward and self-conscious.

Interesting also are Muffat's assertions that certain situations demand certain ornaments, or exclude certain ornaments:

> If one ascends by step, the *appoggiatura* is added to the good notes, either by itself or with a *mordant*. If the notes are too fast, this manner is saved for the slower good notes, when next they come.
>
> In ascending leaps, the *appoggiatura* is added to the good notes, either by itself (20) or with a mordant (21).
>
> In cadences, certain notes require a trill, and certain notes reject a trill. The notes which end cadences are seldom given a trill, unless one leaps down a third or descends by step, or comes, with an appoggiatura, to a *mi* or ♮.
>
> An ascending leap of a third is best relieved by an ascending *exclamation*, which is used by the Lullists only in this place, and elsewhere hardly at all.

These particular cases in which ornamentation was considered by Muffat to be an essential part of the French style are summarized at the end of his section on ornamentation in this way:

> It is therefore essential that one have such diligence in using these valuable musical graces (wherever they are appropriate), such care as to discern where they belong, and such agility as to express them beautifully, that the slightest omission of the *appoggiatura* in ascending passages, or of *trills* on *mi* or ♮ (at least on the good notes), as well as the

---

[4] Comparisons of Muffat's discussion of ornamentation with that of other sources, such as Bacilly, must wait for a future study.

slightest *trill* on a leap, the slightest misuse of the *exclamation* elsewhere than learned, or
the slightest difficulty in playing such figures quickly, fluently, and carefully, will soon
betray those who are not sufficiently experienced in this style, but who have long
imagined themselves to have ascended to the mountaintop of Lullian perfection.

The other ornaments are described in terms which make them optional, although Muffat did
provide examples of passages with tasteful ornamentation. Again, Muffat's clear explanation
on this subject requires little elaboration.

General Conventions

Repeats

In *Florilegium Primum*, Muffat discussed repeat signs and first and second endings in a somewhat confusing manner; however, the music itself is straightforward and performers should
have no trouble knowing how to handle repeats. One statement, however, refers to a practice
of playing each strain more than twice:

> However, I found the practice of some to be not unpleasant, which is to repeat still a third
> time, beginning from the aforementioned sign after the second part has been played
> completely. The musicians should decide this before the performance.

Wendy Hilton has noted that *danses à deux*, the most important type of court dance (which
included the most popular Baroque dance forms), usually lasted from two to three minutes per
couple and were choreographed to specific music.[5] Thus, depending on the length of a particular piece, more time might be required for the choreography than would result from two
iterations of each strain.

Muffat also mentioned repeats in the Foreword of *Auserlesene Instrumentalmusik*:

> . . . the serious Arias are repeated only twice, the more lively ones occasionally three
> times, and the Graves not at all.

By Arias, Muffat meant both movements called *Aria* and movements called by names of
dances. These movements normally are written in binary form with repeats. Movements
marked Grave, however, normally appear between dance-like movements, and are notated
without repeats.

In the case of "more lively" movements in which one can "repeat still a third time" by beginning again "from the aforementioned sign after the second part has been played completely," perhaps what is meant is that once a movement has been played normally, that is,
AABB, one can make a third iteration by playing another AB. In light of Muffat's statement
that "nothing is so splendid . . . if it is heard too often," this might be a more musically desirable approach than forming three iterations by playing AAABBB.

---

[5] Wendy Hilton, "Dance of Court & Theater: The French Noble Style 1690–1725," in *Dance and Music
of Court and Theater: Selected Writings of Wendy Hilton*, Dance & Music Series, No. 10 (Stuyvesant,
NY: Pendragon, 1997), p. 12.

Tempo and rhythm

In the Foreword to *Florilegium Primum*, Muffat discussed the relative tempi of various dances and other movements, and how different time signatures signal different tempi. Experience, he wrote in *Florilegium Secundum*, is the best guide to proper tempi:

> To become acquainted with the proper tempo of the Ballets, what helps the most, other than regular practice with the Lullists, is an understanding of the art of the dance, in which most Lullists are well versed. That is why one should not be amazed at their exact observance of that tempo.

Muffat wrote that tempo is one of the five critical aspects of the French style:

> Third, one must always be aware of the true tempo, or the time and measure, appropriate to each piece. (F2, Remarks)

In the section of *Florilegium Secundum* which deals with tempo (First Remarks, III *Tempus*), Muffat's remarks amount to various pleas not to rush through the dances. Even in very lively dances, one is to "make haste slowly" and to "adhere more to moderation than to haste."
    Muffat complained about a practice which was apparently popular:

> To avoid the errors which violate these two rules, one must first reject the abuse being spread by many, in which every piece, indiscriminately, is performed slowly the first time, faster the second time, and quite rushed the third time.

Both *Florilegia* refer to the French practice of rhythmic inequality; in fact, Muffat, like Loulié, Hotteterre, and François Couperin,[6] describes inequality as the dotting of odd-numbered notes (unlike writers such as Quantz,[7] who described inequality as a *slight* lengthening of odd-numbered notes). The note values which are to be played unequally, "when time allows," are those which are two levels faster than beats; in other words, in meters such as **2** or ¢, which have half-note beats, eighth notes would be played unequally, and in meters such as $\frac{2}{4}$, which have quarter-note beats, sixteenth notes would be played unequally.[8]

---

[6] Betty Bang Mather, *Dance Rhythms of the French Baroque: A Handbook for Performance*, Music: Scholarship and Performance, ed. Thomas Binkley (Bloomington: Indiana University Press, 1987), pp. 139–42.

[7] Quantz, Johann Joachim,*Versuch einer Anweisung die Flöte traversiere zu spielen* (Berlin: Johann Friedrich Boß, 1752; facsimile ed., Wiesbaden: Breitkopf & Härtel, 1988), p. 105.

[8] Mather, pp. 57–66.

Chapter 9

On German Performance Practice

*A*lthough Muffat's intent was to inform his readers about the performance of French and Italian music, scattered among his instructions are hints about the way music was performed in Germany during his lifetime. These hints generally occur in a context of admonition *not* to play in the usual German manner; nevertheless, they offer a glimpse at German musical sensibilities in the late seventeenth century.

It is clear that Muffat considers German violinists to be at least the equals of non-Germans in terms of technique, and that the music which they were accustomed to playing tended to be virtuosic (as witnessed, indeed, by the music of German composers such as Biber, Walther, Schmeltzer, Westhoff, and others). In *Florilegium Primum* he wrote:

> Since the ballet compositions of the above-mentioned Lully, or other such composers, because of their flowing and natural motion, completely avoid irregular runs, frequent and ill-sounding leaps, and all other artifice, they had the misfortune to be at first poorly received in these countries by many of our violinists, who at that time were more interested in the number of unusual devices and artifices in the music than in grace.

The implication is that violin music of late seventeenth-century Germany was characterized by those qualities which the Lullian composers "completely avoid," and French-style music might therefore have been seen by German violinists as uninteresting. (This attitude still exists today among some young, highly proficient players, who react with disdain to technically unchallenging music.)

Florilegium Secundum also contains a reference to the technical prowess of German violinists, in considerably more conciliatory terms than the passage quoted above:

> If [German violinists] were to add the lively, graceful Lullian charm to the musical confidence, agility of the hands, and multitude of virtuosic effects over which they already possess mastery, they would not only equal the foreigners, but would easily surpass them.

Muffat makes a surprising statement about the German manner of holding the bow:

Most Germans agree with the Lullists on the holding of the bow for the violins and violas; that is, pressing the thumb against the hair and laying the other fingers on the back of the bow.

This type of bow-hold is generally associated with France, before Corrette and the popularity of Italian-style violin technique among French violinists; but Muffat offers us evidence that the "thumb-under" hold was used in seventeenth-century Germany as well.

The widespread use of a systematic approach to bowing was apparently confined to France in the seventeenth century, and Muffat's writings support that conclusion. Unlike the musicians of a French orchestra, according to Muffat, the musicians of a German orchestra did not all use the same bowings:

> It is well-known that the Lullists, whom the English, Dutch, and many others are already imitating, all bow the most important notes of the measure . . . in the same way, even if a thousand of them were to play together. Thus when noble men returned to our lands from these places, and did not find this unanimity among our German violinists, who were otherwise excellent, they noticed the difference in the concord of sound and were amazed. (F2, Remarks)

Indeed, a different æsthetic seemed to be operating in Germany; unlike the French musicians, who were concerned with indicating meter and the movements of dance, German musicians looked more to features such as agogics to determine strong and weak inflections (and thus bowings):

> Those who indiscriminately play the first note of a measure up-bow (as often happens among the Germans and Italians in triple time, especially if the first note is shorter than those following) are in direct conflict with the Lullian way of playing. (F2, II *Plectrum*)

Muffat makes several intriguing statements about the German approach to tempo and rhythm. It seems clear (if unsurprising) that Germans did not employ rhythmic inequality as the French did, performing notes notated as equal notes with long/short rhythms.[1] However, a remark in the section *Tempus* from *Florilegium Secundum* cautions against changing the tempo in the middle of a piece:

> Not everyone can hold a set beginning tempo with constant steadiness for as long as a piece is played, and many fail to do so in part or in whole. . . . One errs in part when one measure is played faster than the others, or when one note is played faster or slower than its value demands.

It may be that Muffat was reacting to amateurs' failure to play in a steady tempo. However, this passage could also be a reference to the manner in which professional German violinists were

---

[1] Although German performance practice did not include a convention of rhythmic alteration, one must not assume that notes notated as equal were played to sound all the same. For example, German sources (including Muffat—see *Florilegium Secundum*, example Oo) discuss "good" and "bad" notes.

accustomed to playing. Much of the German solo violin repertoire of the time includes fantastic, improvisatory writing which seems to demand a great deal of freedom in terms of tempo and note values; this passage may be documentary of such a practice, since a violinist accustomed to playing improvisatory music may have balked at playing with the exact precision and metric predictability which Muffat says is crucial to dance music.

On the other hand, despite the freedom of rhythm and tempo with which German violinists may have played, a passage in *Auserlesene Instrumentalmusik* reveals that German tempi were generally more moderate than those of the Italians:

> . . . passages marked with the words *Adagio, Grave, Largo,* et cetera are taken much more slowly than our musicians would play, sometimes to such an extent that one can hardly believe it. However, those marked *Allegro, Vivace, Presto, Più Presto* and *Prestissimo* are taken much livelier and faster.

Chapter 10

Performance Settings

$\mathcal{In}$ each publication, Muffat mentions the uses for which his compositions are intended, or the uses to which they have been put. What is significant about this information is the fact that it tells us about the practical nature of the music contained in those publications — Muffat did not intend his pieces to serve only an academic function, illustrating the principles of performance practice which he described, but were truly written to be performed. The distinction is one of attitude, and is a significant one.

The suites of the *Florilegia*, wrote Muffat, are appropriate as concert music, as "background" music, and as music for dancing:

> These pieces were favorably performed with full harmony for the entertainment of distinguished guests at certain celebrations of the most esteemed Court of Passau, as well as for the dancing practice of the noble youth. (*Florilegium Secundum*, title page)

"Full harmony" no doubt refers to performances with all five parts (since the Quinta Parte was optional).

> [This work] contains no small number of those Ballets newly composed by me in Passau, and which were heard with approval in this esteemed Court both at the dance and when played on several instruments. It owes its origin as much to His Esteemed Grace's forceful zeal for the training of the noble youth of the royal household, as to my desire to please the ear, although they have also served various other purposes, such as chamber music, table music, and night music. (*Florilegium Secundum*, Foreword)

Performances "on several instruments" must refer to concert performance (since it is contrasted with performance at the dance) using a large ensemble. "Chamber music" was a performance by a small ensemble in the private rooms of the ruler; "table music" is music played during a meal; and "night music" was a concert performance between dinner and retiring. The *Florilegia* suites, then, were appropriate for nearly every occasion except in church.

The concerti of *Auserlesene Instrumentalmusik*, according to Muffat, are purely concert music, and are appropriate for all the same settings as the *Florilegia* suites, with the exception of dances:

> This work is . . . quite suitable for the entertainment of the connoisseur, the cheer of social gatherings, and for dinner music and serenades. (AI, title page)

> These concertos, since they were composed only for the particular delight of the ear, can be most fittingly performed for (above all) the amusement of great Princes and Lords, and for the entertainment of prominent guests, grand meals, serenades, and gatherings of music-lovers and virtuosi; they are suitable neither for the Church, because of the ballets and other arias which they contain, nor for dancing, because of the alternation of slow and tragic passages with lively and nimble ones. (*Auserlesene Instrumentalmusik*, Foreword)

The "connoisseur" and "music-lovers" referred to are amateur musicians, as opposed to professionals or "virtuosi."

Conclusion

$\mathcal{T}$he importance of Georg Muffat as a composer and writer cannot be overestimated. A cosmopolitan musician whose musical tastes were as eclectic as his own background, Muffat lived during a period of great changes in the musical landscape of Europe, changes wrought by the advent of new wind instruments in France, by shifting political climates, and by a growing interest in the very styles of music that he helped introduce to Germany, the French and Italian styles. Muffat's own compositions anticipated the movement led by François Couperin to unite the musical styles of France and Italy in a single musical vocabulary; they very successfully combine the grace of one with the power of the other, while at the same time managing to say something very original.

As musicians of the twentieth century whose approach to baroque music seeks to be historically informed, it is our good fortune that Muffat's efforts to promote this union of styles on a large scale resulted in the publications on which this document is based. Admittedly, questions can be asked about how representative of French music of the seventeenth century Muffat's writings actually are, considering the fact that the *Florilegia* were published thirty years after his study in Paris in his teen years. In fact, other writers' descriptions of French performance practice are similar but not identical to Muffat's.[1] But this document has purposefully left those issues, and the comparison studies they would require, for another time, another project.

It is my hope that this document will fulfill Thomas Binkley's desire to make Muffat's writings more accessible to and more fully understood by musicians today. I believe that understanding Muffat's writings can be of great benefit in the quest to achieve a meaningful and practical approach to the performance of French and Italian baroque instrumental music; certainly I have found it so. In the words of Muffat,

Farewell, and wish him well who has attempted to deserve your favor.

---

[1] See, for example, Michel Pignolet de Montéclair (*Méthode facile pour apprendre à jouer du violon*, 1711–12) on bowing rules, and Bénigne de Bacilly (*Remarques curieuses sur l'art de bien chanter*, 1668) on ornamentation.

Bibliography

Barbour, Murray J. *Tuning and Temperament: A Historical Survey*. East Lansing, MI: Michigan State College Press, 1953.

Baumann, H. *Muret-Sanders Encyclopedic English-German and German-English Dictionary*. Part II: German-English. Abridged Version. New York: Murray Printing Company/Ungar Publishing Company, 1931.

Boyden, David D. *The History of Violin Playing from its Origins to 1761*. Oxford: Oxford University Press, 1964; Clarendon Press, 1990.

Carter, Stewart. "Instructions for the Violin from an Overlooked Source: Bartolomeo Bismantova's *Compendio Musicale* (1677)." Ms. From the author, 1998.

Cooper, Kenneth, and Julius Zsako. "Georg Muffat's Observations on the Lully Style of Performance." *The Musical Quarterly* 53 (April 1967):220–245.

Daverio, John. "In Search of the Sonata da Camera Before Corelli." *Acta Musicologica* 57 (February 1985):195–214.

Durant, Will, and Ariel Durant. *The Age of Reason Begins*. The Story of Civilization, Part VII. New York: Simon and Schuster, 1961.

———. *The Age of Louis XIV*. The Story of Civilization, Part VIII. New York: Simon and Schuster, 1963.

Eppelsheim, J. *Das Orchester in den Werken Jean-Baptiste Lullys*. Tutzing: Verlag Hans Schneider, 1961.

Grimm, Jacob, and Wilhelm Grimm. *Deutsches Wörterbuch*. Leipzig: S. Hirzel Verlag, 1877.

Harris, Simon. "Lully, Corelli, Muffat and the Eighteenth-Century Orchestral String Body." *Music and Letters* 54 (April 1973):197–202.

Haynes, Bruce. "Pitch Standards in the Baroque and Classical Periods." Ph.D. diss., Université de Montréal, 1995.

Hilton, Wendy. *Dance and Music of Court and Theater: Selected Writings of Wendy Hilton*. Dance & Music, no. 10. Stuyvesant, NY: Pendragon Press, 1997.

Kolneder, Walter. *Georg Muffat zur Aufführungspraxis*. Strasbourg: Verlag Heitz, 1970.

Marx, Hans Joachim. *Die Überlieferung der Werke Arcangelo Corellis*. Supplemental vol. to *Arcangelo Corelli: Historisch-Kritische Gesamtausgabe der musikalischen Werke*. Köln: Arno Volk Verlag, 1980.

Mather, Betty Bang. *Dance Rhythms of the French Baroque: A Handbook for Performance*. Music: Scholarship and Performance, ed. Thomas Binkley. Bloomington: Indiana University Press, 1987.

McEvedy, Colin. *The Penguin Atlas of Modern History (to 1815)*. London: Penguin Books, 1972.

Messinger, Heinz. *Langenscheidt's New College German Dictionary*. Berlin: Langenscheidt KG, 1973.

Meyer, E. H. *Die Mehrstimmige Spielmusik des 17. Jahrhunderts in Nord- und Mitteleuropa*. Kassel: Bärenreiter, 1934.

Praetorius, Michael. *Die Organographia*. Syntagma musicum, vol. 2. Wolfenbüttel: Elias Holwein, 1619; facsimile ed., Kassel: Bärenreiter, 1985.

———. *Termini musici*. Syntagma musicum, vol. 3. Wolfenbüttel: Elias Holwein, 1619; facsimile ed., Kassel: Bärenreiter, 1988.

Quantz, Johann Joachim. *Versuch einer Anweisung die Flöte traversiere zu spielen.* Berlin: Johann Friedrich Boß, 1752; facsimile ed., Wiesbaden: Breitkopf & Härtel, 1988.

Salzburger Bachgesellschaft. "Biber und Muffat: Salzburger Komponisten zur Zeit des Hochbarock." In *Jahresschrift 1980 der Salzburger Bachgesellschaft.* Salzburg: H. Gattermair Verlag, 1980.

Snyder, Kerala J. *Dieterich Buxtehude: Organist in Lübeck.* New York: Schirmer Books, 1987.

Stampfl, Inka. *Georg Muffat Orchesterkompositionen.* Passau: Verlag Passavia, 1984.

Strunk, Oliver. *Source Readings in Music History.* New York: W. W. Norton, 1950.

Walther, Johann Gottfried. *Musikalisches Lexikon.* Leipzig: Wolffgang Deer, 1732; facsimile ed., Kassel: Bärenreiter, 1953.

Wasielewski, Joseph Wilhelm von. *Die Violine im 17. Jahrhundert.* Bonn: M. Cohen & Sohn, 1874.

Contributors

Professor Thomas Binkley was a noted lutenist and director of early-music performances. He founded the Early Music Institute at the Indiana University School of Music.

Dr. Ingeborg Harer is Assistant Professor at the Institut für Musik und darstellende Kunst in Graz, Austria.

Dr. Ernest Hoetzl is Assistant Professor of Pedagogy at the Universität für Musik und darstellende Kunst in Graz, Austria.

Dr. Yvonne Luisi-Weichsel teaches in the pedagogy department of the Universität für Musik und darstellende Kunst in Graz, Austria.

Dr. David K. Wilson is a baroque violinist based in the San Francisco area. He has taught Baroque violin at Indiana University and has performed extensively with period instrument chamber ensembles and orchestras in the United States and Europe.